ON THE BEACH

Poems 2016 – 2021

ON
THE
BEACH

Poems 2016 – 2021

ALAN
WELTZIEN

Cirque Press

Copyright © 2022 Alan Weltzien

Published by Cirque Press

Sandra Kleven — Michael Burwell
3157 Bettles Bay Loop
Anchorage, AK 99515

Print ISBN: 979-8-88757-900-9

cirquejournal@gmail.com
www.cirquejournal.com

Cover photograph - "Sea Grass" by Jim Thiele
Author photograph by Alan Weltzien
Book Design by Emily Tallman, Poetica

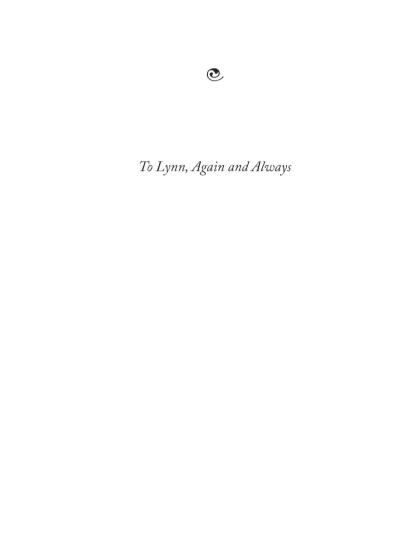

To Lynn, Again and Always

ACKNOWLEDGMENTS

Thanks to the following journals or anthologies where poems in this book were previously published: *Cirque, Cloudbank, From Whispers to Roars (The Climax), Nine Cloud Journal, Oakwood, Poetry in the Time of Coronavirus, The Limberlost Review, The Spirit It Travels: An Anthology of Transcendental Poetry, The Sea Letter, We Take Our Stand: Montana Writers Protecting Public Lands, Whitefish Review.*

CONTENTS

Section IV.
Distant Geographies

INTRODUCTION

Ruud by Nature

In *The San Francisco Call* (12/13/1898) column, Elias Ruud's mustache droops into his goatee, obscures his mouth. His close-set eyes and swirl of hair combed neatly right, nondescript mugshot at the 19th-century's end. Just a regular guy. Three pen drawings of "The Three Leading Characters" in the real-life Ibsen drama, with Camilla Nielsen poised between Ruud, her lover, and suffering husband, Jorgen, descend in a diagonal, with Ruud's rectangle placed midway through the column.

Should I blame Ibsen, that rabble-rousing dramatist with thick muttonchops and cigar who punctured the status quo and whom I've read and taught for decades? Or should I blame Ruud, who worked on a radical paper, *From* ("Forward"), in Fredrikstad until he was chased away, and who acted in amateur productions in San Francisco?

The headlines, in decreasing font, blare "IBSEN CAST A FATAL SPELL O'ER HER LIFE," "'Doll's House' is Deserted," "NIELSEN DIVORCE ROMANCE," and "Wronged Spouse Claims His Pretty Erring Wife Was Hypnotized by Elias Ruud and the Norwegian Poet."

We smack our lips over the old human triangle, another instance of soured Danish-Norwegian relations since Camilla, Dane wife, played Solveig to wandering Peer Gynt, played by Ruud, an insurance agent, married man, and father of three children including my grandfather, Ollie. Peer/Elias, also playing Don Juan, seduced Camilla, mother of two daughters who lost her usual high spirits and confessed to Jorgen. He lays the entire blame upon Ruud whom, he claims, has hypnotized her and turned her brain with "Ibsen logic."

The old wizard with bushy beard and pince-nez turns heads again.

Camilla believed it was impossible for her to live without him and like Nora Helmer, protagonist of Ibsen's *A Doll's House*, had a higher duty and that was duty to herself. Jorgen sang "Norwegian Wood," final verse. This bird has flown.

We read Ruud's reputation in the Norwegian community is a most unsavory one as he'd flirted with bigamy years earlier. He risked the New World/new wife plot but his marriage to a young woman was called off at the altar when his wife and daughters were discovered in the old country, ready to sail. Ooops.

Following her lover's advice Camilla invested $300 in a little stationery store but after two weeks, turned over to Mrs. Ruud the shop and the furniture she had received from Nielsen, then sailed north to Tacoma and the Klondike with fevered Peer. You get the shop, I get the man. Chase women, chase gold.

Mrs. Mary Ruud, schoolteacher and faithful wife, files a suit for divorce ten days before the scandal broke. She rescues her young son from orphanage front steps and soon she and the kids sail north too, third-class steerage, to join Seattle's Norwegian community. She knows no one, ends up dressing hair for wealthy Seattle women. A painter, Oscar Weltzien, follows her, marries in a few years, adopts Ruud's children. He paints her and her portrait hangs above my easy chair and she smiles sturdily over our sunroom. A framed photo hangs above my bureau and she grits her teeth in a forced smile. Oscar's photo hangs a few inches away. A few wrinkles frame her eyes and mouth. Every morning I stare at her set face. How did she endure her wayward first husband, go it alone after his final exit?

When Elias visits in Seattle, he calls his daughters and son "my little friends." Maybe he took *Peer Gynt* to heart, as he proved a better actor than father. But for his rude conduct I'd be Ruud and I've already been accused of that.

Section I.

HIGH AND DRY

PALL

Mid-August, wildfire smoke settles like a heavy quilt over the
rolling flats, blocks the sun. Hurtling down to the Columbia, I
plunge into an acrid soup and swim east as I inhale sharp smoke,
search in vain for blue. I scan the white blur, sagebrush not quite
clear, control my breath inside the air-conditioned car. Spokane's
towers waver in a wasteland, "hazardous" air quality for days.

At the Continental Divide the sun spokes the ground and farther
east familiar hills nod in familiar places, the Clark Fork winks
a time or two, my lungs relax as the burned smell dissipates.
The Flint Creek range opens, but in the "new norm" I await the
next visitation of summer's foul breath that pours and sinks:
a democratic curse that rubs out sightlines and spoils August,
formerly Big Sky's showcase now lost in thick haze.

LANDSCAPE WITHOUT FIGURES: FROM HIGHWAY 278 EASTBOUND AFTER BADGER PASS, MONTANA

Just beyond a chute fringed by lodgepole
the roadbed rises then breasts, sagebrush
clumps forever and the Beaverhead Valley
unrolls, widening ripples in a giant pond,
girded by near and distant ranges with local

names tagged to memory. Somewhere in this
broad brown bowl capped by winter snow
a river runs through it and borders the town
called home this quarter century, invisible
in the big round view where riparian zones

retreat to mountain shoulders and sheds
or houses, infrequent, shrink below vision
and what's changed since William Clark
and crew trod through and long before
them, Shoshone hunted and fished? Where

is the crowded 21st century in this Montana
panorama, this wide-angle basin and range?
Where am I, a dot between wagging sagebrush?
Novelist Thomas Savage said, "It's impossible…
to look at the horizon…and consider that there

is such a thing as Europe or neighbors or
anything else." Big Sky Country shrinks a guy,
enfolds me within countless open benches
and ridges. Standing on a mountaintop,
growing tiny amidst a jumble of aspiring

points, I lose myself in the curving rim
without end that cups my middle life.

DRY FLIES

— for Adam Hutchison

Adam, my former student, reads the riffles and snags
as he dips oars and pivots his driftboat's bow or stern
and advises Tom, my old friend, and me where to present
our flies. Each turn in the river holds more stories
that spring from Adam's box of memories, of deep

familiarity with his favorite Montana river. He quotes
his brother's credo: "I'd rather catch one decent
trout on the Big Hole than fifteen on the Beaverhead."
Braced in the bow, Tom, who hasn't fished in eleven
years, casts with widening arcs and grace, presenting

his fly within inches of shore grasses or in a side
channel's still pool. I cast with or without a bobber,
follow Adam's advice and still the surges of laughter
at myself as the student compliments his aging teacher:
"You've got the hang of it, Doc!" Tom catches a whitefish

then a rainbow then a brookie, and he plays several
more, his rod hungry. I squint, occasionally lose the fly
in the flash of the lowering sun. I decide one can either
fish or drink beer and watch birds and shorelines
and hills beyond, and after my final tangle, my fly

unswallowed, I reel in, prop my rod, finish another
beer, quote Norman Maclean again, and surrender
to the sinking sun, the gather of dusk. I follow the swoop
of swifts, the rising shadowline on McCartney Mountain,
and the river's music, a chorus of sibilant voices that rise
as our day quiets to night.

HALF MOON PARK ON THE FOURTH OF JULY

— for Scott Friskics

No Roman candles or cherry bombs this holiday;
sifting breezes pour off the steep scarp which
scallops and dimples, a giant stone smile, full-
lipped and bowed like a fat Cupid's or a painted
flapper's, with bulging curves before each
retreating corner and in the center of its pursed
upper lip, a convex ridge to kiss. Far above,
the squat knob of Scapegoat Mountain's summit
crowns the massif and below the billowing
curtain we pitch our tent, recline on hillside
grasses between spikes of fading balsamroot,
stare and smile back at the tall wall whose
waves bend more than a half moon's round.

Later I study the Lewis Thrust Belt, imagine
in time lapse those sedimentary layers west
of the faults that slide up and over layers
to the east, fat slabs that crest and crash
and freeze as exposed reefs. As Scott and I
walk along Half Moon Park's center below
its slightly parted lips, slender commas
of spray curl out, backlit, from unseen
recesses and puff into mist, a sign like
the low cave at Delphi though I can't fathom
its mystery, only the pulse of plunging
water fed by invisible snow, breaths of wind.

The wall undulates, the Park's broad
amphitheater pitches and rolls, and I search

for other signs on the nation's birthday, traces
of movement just beyond eye and ear. Two
days later we backpack along Cave Creek
Pass just beyond the smile as wet snow swirls,
dusts our heads and green meadows.

BETWIXT

— for Scott

As my friend reads
an explication of the *Heart*
Sutra I watch a woodpecker
on a dead trunk jutting
above Wrong Creek.
It never pecks, barely
perches and peers before
it flashes up then dives
towards the Creek
or flutters away only
to return. It neither
stays nor abandons
its chosen post, lands
only to leave then
arrive, a sprite forever
back
        and
                forth.

The dance between stasis
and flight, home and away.
The pecker quits
its fleet pattern and flies off.

ANCIENT AGE

— for Alec

In Great Basin National Park
decades ago
I ignore the closed trail sign
and stomp through spotty drifts of snow,
my older son matching my steps.
We enter the bristlecone pine grove
and silence,
pause before a tree whose sign
proclaims 3,200 years old
and time slips in the altitude.
I no longer hear my watch
or the afternoon
when I try to explain the world's
oldest tree
to a boy no longer a child
who later majors in history.
I cannot walk centuries or millennia
to connect
this gnarled relic more dead than alive
whose bristle brush stems,
yellow green,
shimmer, tease our eyes
which scan the dolomitic slope.
I bow, grateful for the audience,
and we step back into the day
as transient as our visit
and our lives.

GHOST FOREST

— for Scott Friskics and Jim McLean

We trudge down the North Fork drainage,
no live trees in sight, only a simulacrum
forest where dead trees rise shorn of most
branches. Scott says, "In the Bob Marshall
you see lots of burns and lots of stands
like this." For days we've walked through

open woods whose thick green mat
of wildflowers offsets the stark landscape
at eye level and above, wide swaths
of stripped trees whose trunks may not
be scorched and who sway and creak
as though, tall and naked, they remain

what they no longer are, admit wide
sprays of sunlight through missing
canopies: a child's stick forest, a
minimalist imitation beyond scattered
scraggly limbs and beyond needles
or leaves, a new species of woods

in a warming time, mute reminder
of their barked and fluid cambium past.
We pant in afternoon heat, search
for shade beneath non-trees which
loom everywhere until, with enough time
and wind, gravity completes their

funeral obsequies and we scramble
over and through deadfall, jumbled
in crazy angles, a jutting graveyard,
helter skelter pile-up that buries trails
and impedes our way: testimony of logs
once trees, spaced, each reaching its
patch of sky.

HEAVY METAL

Shifting cues delay migrations;
a snowstorm pushes 3,000
snow geese into Berkeley Pit's

anti-lake, "a 50 billion-gallon
toxic stew," to water and feed
and die. Flat surface below,

ochre tiers curve and twist,
a poisonous tide surge
governed by no moon; the water,

unlike any other, beckons
birds. A Siren trap that folds
their broad white wings: angelic

canaries in the open pit
remnant of the mines, yawning
maw that ate East Butte. Whose

wet gorge rises.

EARTH DAY 2018

At the Divide exit I step with a dozen
others, orange highway vests snug,
as our eyes scan the short grasses
and hands reach down, seize plastic
spoons, styrofoam cup pieces, beer
bottles whole or broken, soda cans
round or smashed, cigarette butts,
blown tractor trailer tire strands,
frayed waving plastic bags, candy
wrappers, torn shirts or shorts:
spent ejecta casually tossed.

Snowfields on Fleecer Mountain
and other tops shine down on our
mundane cleansing. Warm breeze
lifts my vest's edge and when I
draw near the highway shoulder
trucks and vans bullet past. Their
fast Doppler effect buffets my body.
I remember highway clean-ups
along our town's north border.
I sing the old chorus: people
are pigs but in saying so, pigs
get a bad rap.

What disconnections explain those
easy discards from passing windows?
What gaps invite that flick-of-the-
wrist? Is it garbage in garbage out?
Out of sight out of mind? We litter
away some piece of personal
responsibility, one that gleams

like a gem in Germany or Japan
where I see no leavings. Trash slides
ineluctably from verb to noun
and our work this day retards
briefly growing lines of garbage
along highways and rivers and the
floating mountains beyond them.

Those trace elements of our passing
fade far slower than ourselves,
pock the borders of lanes and lives,
bob and blob our oceans, mute
reminders of our indifference, a tide
that rises faster than our care.

THE GIANT ABOVE THE GATES: HELENA, MONTANA

— for Wayne Chamberlin

1.
Approaching Sleeping Giant

The Giant slumbers on his back like a stiff-armed mummy
or a nobleman's funeral monument in a cathedral side aisle,
head east, torso west, and the big head and nose recall
Alfred Hitchcock's publicity stunt advertising *Frenzy*
when he floats on the Thames and tilts his massive head
to address us in sepulchral, doleful tones as he gently bobs.
This stone giant just north of the Prickly Pear Valley does not
wink as our group threads past the Synness Ranch (Est. 1876)
homestead, a squat suite of cabins and sheds surrounded,
in early June, by tall grass, meadows punctuated with
perennials. The outhouse has a fresh roll. We angle up
past the final gate, locate the trail and public land boundary,
take aim for his head. The city rises much farther away
than it is: the old Big Sky story of remoteness just beyond
a town's last street, the end of pavement. The Giant inhabits
another country beyond Helena.

2.
On The Nose

It's not every day one can crawl up a giant's nose
which turns out to be two noses, broad rock spires,
that blend as one in the viewshed. The group rises
with the day's heat along the trail which, like the slope,
steepens amidst rockslides, sage, a lone pine or two

that throws a narrowing circle of shade. Three of us
scramble ahead, stairstep clefts and even our breaths
on top as we track the panorama to the south. Later
we spot the others, daunted by high-angle rock.
We snack lazily, count mountain ranges under the
sky's dome. The nose's point, like any vantage in
Montana high country, unfolds more views than
we can absorb in a day or a life.

3.
Above the Gates

But my eyes keep returning to the Missouri River 2,000 feet
below in its broad oxbow just below Meriwether Lewis's
Gates of the Mountains. Boat wakes, silent, unzip silver-
white seams in the flat surface, slow curves in the oxbow.
Just here a river runs through the Rockies in geology's
eternal dance between uplift and erosion, Mission Canyon
Limestone and the mighty Mo which, newly released,
has a long way to flow, northeast and east and southeast
and south, draining the continent to its bottom beyond
New Orleans. Here, Norman Maclean writes, "catastrophes
everywhere enfold us as they do the river" but disaster,
the earth's or ours, feels infinitely more remote than
Montana backcountry this calm day where a motley
crew smiles as they take stock of the vistas and perhaps
of themselves. The view out lights the view in.
Every panorama deepens the love affair.

RUTTISH

High in tundra land
  off Rocky Mountain National
    Park's Trail Ridge Road

a bull tosses his rack,
  snorts, paws hard and
    dirt flies as he

squirms down but he cannot,
  instead he leaps up
    twists and turns

his body not his own
  in this manic dance
    marked by falling

light and temperature, sex
  show for dozens
    gripped by his antic

fit. As he gyrates, cars shudder
  and when he bugles
    the peaks bow.

DEATH VALLEY SEXTET

1.
Moonburst

Thick mats of stars pummel our heads,
stir our deep desire for the night sky,
ancient solace. We face east at the Furnace Creek
oasis in Death Valley, an official dark park.
No student has witnessed such a stellar
show with the Milky Way,
a wide blanket draped across the middle.

Well before the waning winter moon
breaks the crest of the Funeral Mountains,
trumpets blow a fanfare. Widening rays
of moonlight, a radial baroque sunburst,
splay the sky from south to north, eclipse
the Way and announce the moon.
Overhead, a pair of beacons cloud,
ripple like sand dunes at Mesquite Wells,

quicken bright light and the moon, after the long
drumroll, lifts swiftly off a notch in the black
ridge, anti-climax following the laser
show that sweeps the sky and hushes
us. We gape, rapt witnesses pulled like a tide
to the luminous plate: Siren mirror with craters
and seas bearing Latin names that pool
our longing and light our way.

2.
Salt Creek Pupfish

In late afternoon's falling heat, we stroll
Salt Creek and track pupfish, so named
by an expert because they play like puppies,
dart upstream
      left to right
and back,
             give chase then
      hover
in eddies of the gentle current and pinpricks
of shade.

Mature at 1 inch, less schooled than minnows,
they flit and I grin and read the story
of their fragile ecology, each variety
only fitted to its tiny salty drainage,
a tenuous hold in a shifting desert.
In the miracle of creeping water in a dry
place, pupfish fin hard, burst ahead,
pellets of speed in their miniscule
niche.

3.
Frolic at Zabriskie Point

Before tourist buses arrive, my students
stand before the plaques, size up the mosaic
of ridges and creases, spread along the marked
bottom trail or footworn tops, take endless

pictures, laugh at this impossible palette

marked by paltry words like beige,
tan, dun, pink, ochre. Did old Zabriskie,
Pacific Coast Borax Company general manager,

ever pause between mule teams to apprehend
endless pillows and fans and tucks and soft
gullies? sniff textures not unlike our
own hues and curves and recesses?

I show Antonioni's *Zabriskie Point*,
with Mark and Daria and other couples
who, nude, thrust and roll and feint, happy
animals at play, the fine dust of these loose

hills a new skin. As one acoustic guitar plays,
my students chuckle and cringe at the naked
pastoral, resist this version of the Point they
trod.

The Point, like the Valley, broadcasts
our small bag of words for colors and shapes
and we sigh, fall back onto generous phrases
like earth tones and folds.

4.
The *Commedia Divina* at Death Valley

Several students and I hurry up
the trail from the parking lot
at Dante's View. We gasp at
the panorama more than altitude.
Two press farther.
I join them on their peak
and we squeal and caper,

shoot the spreading scene
that exceeds our images
and mocks our names
that fall so short.

Lost 49ers crazed by gold
named this lowest valley Death
though it faults and shifts and settles
as strata and water move,
and plants, often dormant, stretch.
In a contrary tale of promotion,
one Charlie Brown led businessmen and Nevada's governor,
eager for the best view and tourism,
to this Black Mountains saddle
in April 1926 near Coffin Peak,
and they invoked the Florentine poet
who pictured Hell
in the rock tumbles
of Provence's *Chaine des Alpilles*.

Dante's Gate of Hell famously intones
"Abandon all hope ye who enter here,"
yet we hoot, stunned by the vertical drama
of ragged rock and salt and snow.
No wannabe miners' despair
over a badass shortcut,
no nine descending circles.
Instead of frozen Judecca, the lowest pit,
the broad swath of Badwater Basin,
swirl of salt, over a mile below,
towards which flanges of Panamint debris fans curl.
Instead of Mount Purgatory, I climb the Panamints
whose ridgeline centers on Telescope Peak
opposite us, twice as high,
snow dusted this winter morning.

Instead of heavenly spheres,
a bumpy, higher profile
of frosted Sierra Nevadas
lines out northwest
including Mount Whitney's block
I once hiked.

In the Christian epic, Dante or you
or I are led by Virgil down and down
then up and out, a long sinuous way.
At Dante's View eyes easily traverse
lowest to highest, redemption in a
sweeping glance.
Hell below enfolds heaven afar.
We descend to the nadir.

5.

Sandwaves

In a Death Valley documentary, one profile
shows how sand dunes boom in high summer,
acoustic monitors strategically positioned:
when researchers sit and slide, their butts set off
shallow sound waves that oscillate to one pitch.

On this cool morning as we fan out,
most aim for the highest star dunes
at Mesquite Wells, eyes and feet open,
no hope of torsos exciting a D or F. On
slip faces, sinuous textures of ripples tell

wind's errant story, as do their firmer
surfaces flecked with feldspar and micas.
A photographer's dream of tan and shadowed

swells and peaks softened by windblown sand,
a background chorus. On the billowing

surfaces, critters' tracks inscribe their
passing just as shoeprints narrate a contrary
story of rise and fall and dispersal. The sand-
waves shape-shift, invite our play like a giant
sandbox, our bodies our toys as we roll and

plunge, as gravity tilts ridges from solid
to liquid. The angle of repose lures us
onward. We breathe hard as grains pack
between toes where dunes crest and spill
slower than we slip and drop,

contrary studies in motion.

6.
Gettin' Down and Around at Ubehebe Crater

"U-bee-he-bee," two trochees, four-
stroke engine or a quatrain
with b, c, d on long ee. For the Timbisha

Shoshone "Tem-pin-ttu-Wo'sah," or Coyote's
Basket, which willing hikers descend, slowly
slip up while more circumambulate.

With a "Maar volcano," rising magma
steams ground water and explodes
up and out just yesterday in geology's

time. "Fanglomerate" layers in oranges
and tans, on east side, offset thick charcoal
layers of cinder below and along the rim.

"Little Hebe" south of Mother Hebe
cups amidst several maar rims
incomplete, which complete the family.

Like a Jules Verne orifice,
Ubehebe pulls some who plunge-stomp
to its beige bottom where our eyes

finger sharp gullies, green leaves
of desert plants. Coyote, naughty
as always, blew up this big deep

basket and lures us to its base
and roughly plaited rim where
we weave up and down, picture
maar bursts as wind buffets us.

CHALK DESSERT

In Oregon's Owyhee River canyon
the guides announce "the cathedral"
as the oarboats pass its prow and
pull into Chalk Basin, a giant tiered

cake whose chocolate layers,
black basalt, offset the vanilla
lake sediment and wet my tongue.
Erosion narrows the upper stripes

of buttes at whose bases hoodoos
lurch like misshapen toadstools.
I want to eat but instead hike up
canyon and butte, my feet

passing above the cocoa strata.
I learn the cake comes from
the "Oregon-Idaho Graben," "a
giant depression" into which

rhyolite flowed repeatedly. I take
comfort in the knowledge that from
such a pit, with enough yeast and
heat and luck, a grand rock torte rises.

THE PRINCESS AND THE BEETLE

Our second afternoon in the Owyhee River
canyon, the group sits at the portable tables
anchored in Chalk Basin's sand. Beer-thirty
though Katinka tells me she only drinks French
champagne which she imports by the pallet.

A day earlier in a hot happy hour, she sits
by herself, her floppy white hat matched
by white pants, no smudges. A young crew
member then my son sit nearby, engage
her before I approach. Katinka, tall

pale Dutch and trophy-wife attractive,
lounges on her own raft and sleeps in her
own tent and nobody intrudes. I learn
more of her past four years as a
grieving young widow, her husband's

success as a trial lawyer, their international
travel. I hear later about the $300,000
Ferrari, her open-ended American journey,
her desire to design a new house that must
be at least 10,000 square feet to house

the European antiques she has collected.
When I ask "who will clean?" she hesitates,
rules out strange hands. But at Chalk
Basin a big black beetle crawls close
to her chair and she rises abruptly

and quits the table. She mutters "I don't
always like the nature," supplying the
definite article as some Europeans do,
and her eyes fill. Another woman and I
hug her and she talks about her dead

husband, how much he loved rafting trips
with this company, how she tries to enjoy
being out there with him. I wonder what
other fears lurk just beyond her white
apparel, her five-carat ring? I wonder

if she can shed her burdens any easier
than her immaculate clothes or whether
her wealth will press her like her wide-
brimmed hat, securely tied? I wonder
if she knows why that beetle, striding

over sand, stripped her open?

IN OUR SKIN

The tall four-year old,
our rafting group's only child,
plays naked in river sand.
He clutches a branch,
squats and draws then charges
elsewhere, talks to imagined
friend or enemy. He requires
no fig leaf, his uncircumcised
penis flops easily. Sand packs
between his buttocks then falls.
He moves easily between his
playmates and his mother
and other adults. He eats
on the run, stops on raft
and when we take out
at trip's end, suffers
clothes. We eye his antics,
our sagging flesh and clothes
an impossible distance from
his glowing skin.

GRANDE RONDE SUITE

— for James Nash

1.
Prelude

North
West Company
voyageurs name it "Great
Wheel" in the early 19th century "because
of [the valley's] circular shape." Though on
the river I don't trace a round. I roll the French r's,
weave through square dance's "grand right and left" as
the raft plunges northwest then northeast then east
from lower Wallowa River past Minam through
Wild and Scenic, tumbles in lower canyon
past stacks of terraced basalt
to Heller Bar on the
Snake and curves
this diamond
into a
circle.

2.
Minuet

A whitetail deer strokes
        across the current, west to east,
                only meters in front of the raft

her dark eyes and nimble legs
        sense an audience, possible predators,
                as she scrambles between short gray scarps

the first route a mistake
          when she tips backward, feet to sky,
                    yet lands on all fours, a cat;

as the raft draws abreast, a frisson of fear
          ripples her muscles on a second
                    chute of soil between rock

and she gains altitude and safety,
          a more composed fluid trot
                    while I silently applaud downriver

3.
Air

The morning of our last camp
short miles above Boggan's Oasis,
he spies a blond who forages in shrubs
above the pines behind camp.
"I've only seen four in my life"
admits this lifelong hunter;
neither my son nor I have seen
one. In their color phases, Jim
explains, black bears are sometimes
blonds. Through my binocs his caramel
coat shimmers as he stretches
hindlegs, gorges on leaves and grubs,
wallows about, sniffs for scents, nose
extended, occasionally resorts to four
legs as he shifts a few feet. We stand
in a row, rapt witnesses to a honey
bear who glistens in the day's
young light.

4.
Allemande

In interior Northwest river canyons,
        early season,
syringa, known domestically as Lewis's
        mock orange,
festoons rock outcroppings, cascades towards water's
        edge; thick petal
clusters spill, a floral cornucopia whose sweet scent
        perfumes eddies
where boaters pause before fast high water, inhale
        the essence of spring
from the sturdy plants that reach up and out and down
        in billowing white bunches.

5.
Sarabande

        In the lower Grande Ronde canyon,
        thinning grasses tinctured green in late
        spring, Grande Ronde Basalt
        stacks higher as we drop below 1,000 feet,
        follow the diving water seam that
        exposes layer upon layer, according
      to a WSU geologist "three magnetostrati-
      graphic units and thirty-five flows."
      I roll "Plagioclase-phyric flows. . .
    with thick entablatures" around
    my mouth, geology's unwieldy
    word-lumps as I taste an ocher
  layer cake far higher than that eight-
  layer jam cake in Tennessee, tallest
  I've ever et, or discern a more

intricate series of parapets guarding
a larger castle than I've ever seen, or
a series of failed terraces that would
rival any steep stacks in Nepal or Japan
or Indonesia. But cake or castle
or terrace fall short of canyon
as we sink deeper below tiers, test
geology's precision with our tongue
as they loom just above the river's

edge.

6.
Gigue

Near its mouth the Grande Ronde
constricts to less
than half its
width and surges,
two throats
between tumbled
basalt where
we walk
and scout.
A wood
cross above
a cairn,
memento
mori
and this
race's
caution flag.
Jim picks
our line

and in
the raft
we hunker
down
pitch and
yaw
whoop
pound
and slow
below,
wet and grinning
as the River opens wide,
re-composes itself in its
march to its union with the Snake.

At the Narrows, the Grande Ronde River's only Class IV rapid.

FIRE AND FLOOD

In our new norm
                              moisture withdraws
             underground,
desiccated branches limp
                              cured grasses curl
             dirt cracks
cambium slows, ladder fuels
                              bunch, lean
             invite lightning
jags and flames rage up-
                              and downslope
             mock our
boundaries as they push
                              their own
             and smokeclouds
rise and writhe down drainages
                              over divides
             then collect, settle
over valleys where towns and cities
                              spread
             trapped beneath
heavy acrid haze. Weeks pass
                              sightlines smudge
             and thick
smoke blankets swirl in lungs
                              mountains disappear
             familiar worlds eclipsed
by blanched smog bitter
                              on tongue,
             true blue
sky in fleeting patches overhead.

                              Dry thoughts
              in a burned
season that never ends.

One time zone and several
                              degrees south
              wheeling Harvey
heats in the hot Gulf
                              saunters ashore
              hangs around
for days and rain falls
                              in sheets
              Biblical deluge
forty days in five, which
                              drowns flat land
              swells bayous
and rivers so rugs rot
                              mold flowers
              in drywall
and tens of thousands dry out
                              after feet
              of downpour
billions in damage,
                              endless mud,
              swamp thoughts
in a sodden season.

In our new norm no rain
                              for months
              or months
of rain in days. In Montana,
                              Big Smoke
              Country,
we flounder through diffuse
                              sour fog,

             "a toxic
airborne event" marked by
                        red sun
            orange moon,
crisp air a fleeting memory
                        as weeks
            blur
smoke and ash drops
                        like rain
            like Irma
in Florida.

TWO COUNTRIES

1.

My wife and I edge along the shaded lanes,
straight or perpendicular, to park at Fort
Robinson State Park and visit the ghost
of Crazy Horse. Renovated barracks available
for rent burst with vacationers on porches
or picnic tables or over grills. Generations
toss frisbees or drink beer while barbequing
meat teases my nostrils. Park headquarters
and hotel lobby blur as a flow swings
the screen doors to and fro. The 1905
building housing the museum echoes our
footsteps, sole visitors, as the history
of this military outpost unscrolls according
to the 19th-century legacy of conquest.
Bordered by an eroded parapet on the
north, the fort makeover crawls with
civilians at summer leisure whose play
rubs out the companies of soldiers
guarding captive North Cheyenne who
once busted out before another roundup
and capture. No fifes and drums on
these parade grounds, a panorama
of shouts and laughter and ice cream cones.

2.

South of the state highway beyond the main
buildings and traffic, yards before a restored
guardhouse, a square squat fieldstone pillar,
with an inlaid stone tablet set at an angle,
marks what we came for, incised in headlines:

ON THIS SPOT
CRAZY HORSE
OGALLALA CHIEF
WAS KILLED
SEPT. 5 1877

Histories describe a tussle in which the
charismatic leader, under house arrest,
was escorted to this guardhouse though
he wanted to break away to visit his
critically ill wife, and instead met an eager
bayonet. I struggle to imagine this murder
that reprises again the white-brown story
of contact. Faulkner claimed "the past is never
dead. It's not even past," but this short monument
intrudes in the wide blithe country of the present
like an unwelcome foreign emissary, best ignored.
What place does past tragedy claim alongside
horseback rides and hot dogs? Should guilt,
that sour taste, undercut a sweet amnesia?
Better to pretend Faulkner wrong, ignore the mystic
killing of a chief.

BIG SKY COUNTRY

— for Charlie O'Leary and Callie Boyle

Out of Devil's Hole
we angle along steep sage
slopes, our three horses
and packhorse a sure-footed
quartet, and the old Snowcrest
Trail bends north then east
then north and eyes
pivot from thick patches
of white columbine
to endless spaces
with few roads
and fewer sheds
in sight.

Thunder rumbles
and shafts of virga
almost kiss ground.
Elsewhere, local rain,
a narrow white sheen,
drops below purpling
clouds that blow away
from us.

Canyons and flats and ridges
swell beyond recognition
and though we ride high
we diminish,
a moving speck
above endless swaths
of country bereft

of people
and we rise
above broad siege bands,
float above saddles
and sere sage benches,
dance along vistas
we share
with no one.
Problems
like crowds
fade beyond our vision:

in Big Sky Country
the land's scale
shrinks our shadows
mocks our footprint
and we disappear
into distance.

Section II.

ON YOUTH AND AGING

GHOST SISTER

The rare surviving black-and-white photos
show a broad-faced toddler with curls,
legs splayed out, uncertain grin.
In a few shots the round discs of tiny wire-
rim glasses shine. She blinks,

struggles to focus. A sister, named after two
aunts to preside over brothers,
falls short
of her third birthday, never grows
into Wendy from J.M Barrie's Darling clan.

Firstborn, fruit of rubella fever
in Mother's first trimester, whose mid-
century training as a nurse missed
the dark tale of defects, this baby limps
away from the family: bad heart and eyes, slack

muscles, delayed advancement, bursting
bag of problems, dead months
before my arrival. What shadow does
she cast over those who keep one framed
picture in their bedroom? Mom shakes

her head at her own ignorance, tries to slough
off blame; Dad, eyes wet, never mentions it.
I stare at that frame and will her
to life, imagine her seated at table
but her image freezes. She refuses to budge.

Decades later when I play the song
"Our Baby's Book," Mom shudders,
requests, "Please turn that off," and I
hurtle back to bereft parents
whose firstborn slipped from their arms.

When my older son arrives, I sound a shout
from the rooftop. Then Dad's pained silence,
Mom's infrequent explanations
and my lost sister all float
before me, her absence a mute hole.

TELLING TIME

I turn ten the week
of the Cuban missile crisis
and my folks give me
my first wristwatch.

We sit in endzone bleachers
that Saturday for a Huskies
home game. I watch
my watch, tracing

the second hand. Amidst
the shouts I smell adult
fear, see Dad's worry lines.
What's the time?

CATCHER

Back then every boy, able or not,
played Little League, aped America's
game, so I joined the Duke Snyders,
suited up as a Tiger. As catcher I
strained the straps squatting
behind home plate. Coach Gilleland
yelled "hustle hustle hustle!" every
practice and I pistoned my chubby
legs slower than teammates.

Once, when a player on first stole
second base, I hurled the ball
halfway to left field. The Tigers
went 0-8 that season and I've barely
recovered. I held a book better
than a fat catcher's mitt, shed mask
and guard, orange-striped uniform.
Mom liked to chant "hustle hustle
hustle!" and I have, after my fashion,
far from the striped diamond and green field.

THE WHITE PINE STOOL

My hands clutched books not socket wrenches.
I couldn't hammer straight and breathed hard
in Mr. Berntson's required eighth-grade shop
class full of boys, power tools, and sawdust.

My "handy," misshapen lump of three laminated
woods, earned a C, my grade anxiety diluted
my scorn, and Dad and I scanned his *Workbench*
issues until a stool design grabbed a hold of us.

I blinked the "original, independent work"
requirement, cut and sanded and glued,
with Dad's hands, the white pine round top
and pair of legs that fit in a right-angle groove.

The A grade forced a smile and I locked my
guilt in a tiny wood box. How did Dad weigh
his complicity? Years later he painted a
rosemaling design over the top, reinforced

the legs after I sat on the stool, signed it
"Dad 1978." Mom proudly said "the white
pine stool" with only a tincture of irony,
fruit of illicit collaboration when tools

and I were strangers. For decades the stool
sits adjacent to our downstairs couch, wry
reminder of adolescent clumsiness overlain
by Dad's artistry, fragment of family lore.

With varnish over rust paint the stool shines,
especially the decorated top whose scrolling
leaves and flowerets, green and blue
and ochre, reveal his easy brush.

LEARNER'S PERMIT

When I took the wheel in Everett,
the old Ford Galaxie accelerated
sluggishly. When I stopped in the cabin
driveway and my left foot met air
instead of the emergency brake pedal,
already depressed, my cheeks reddened
as I confessed. Dad asked, "Didn't you
smell anything? Burned rubber?"

After dinner I sat behind the wheel
determined to redeem myself.
Down near Camano Head in green light,
no cars for miles, the Ford slowly
drifted across the southbound lane
and settled into the leafy ditch.
Dad asked, "What the hell
were you looking at?" I lamely
piped, "At the trees," watched
the butt of his Penney's Big Mac
pants bounce in dusk as he jogged
off to find a man with tractor and
chain to pull a scatterbrain
out of his fog.

When our kids learned stick shift
on the Mazda 626, I saw Dad's
receding figure on the red screen
of my impatience. My wife volunteered,
weathered the initial jerks, and I
never landed in a ditch.

SWINGER

When I pick up Alison Lamont for junior prom,
sweat already trickles beside my generous stomach.
No partier, I make my debut with my Humanities
teacher's daughter who wears long black hair, curves
in the right places, and bobs forward as she practices
clarinet in the band room, a personal metronome
whose motions somehow intrigue me.

Pressure on after she'd said yes, I rehearse various
lines as we drive to the gym. A thin necktie ties off
my florid face and I hope she doesn't smell my wet
armpits while my fingers sense her warm flesh
beneath the slightly damp dress during the slow
dances, a halting circle of two. My tongue engaged,
I struggle to impress even as I imagine disrobing

her despite fumbling fingers. But I couldn't cross
the gap, stroke her naked body as I fantasized,
paralyzed by shyness, that thick curtain draped
over girls I could not raise. Maybe she waits
for some action, another guy. I buy her a black
garter at Farrell's Old Fashioned Ice Cream Parlour
but don't slide it to her thigh, only ask "How long

is your hair? Eighteen inches?" After the expected
peck on her smooth cheek, I retreat to a weird friend's
house to debrief, my high school dance career over.
Allison later had several kids I heard. I learned to talk
with girls, discovered how much I like to shake it
out there, having shaken off some pounds
and raised that curtain.

GRANDMOTHERS WITHOUT FEAR

"Lady, you're going on *that?*" the man asks
Gram Boos ("oh"), who stands in the roller
coaster line at the Puyallup Fair. "Why sure!"
Her Boston accent bends those vowels.
Silver-white ringlets curl around her round
face and soft brown eyes gleam behind
her glasses. Her 5'2" stocky frame steadies
itself over dark square-heeled shoes. My folks
and select friends call her "Mrs. Plumpso,"
their voices thick with affection.

Gram Boos, formerly Christian Scientist,
uses the "n-" word, calls physicians "damn
doctors," votes for Goldwater, rides chairlifts
and coasters if possible, says "I love the views."
Mom retorts, "I wouldn't be caught dead that
far off the ground!" Gram flew solo to Hawaii just
after statehood and a smiling, brown-skinned
woman gently draped a fresh lei over her head.

The pimply attendant double checks the
restraint as our car lurches forward then
catches a cog and grinds up that steady
endless incline, my pulse races, and we
rise higher than anywhere and poise, giddy,
an improbable second before the vertiginous
plunge that childs us all. We shout through
tight banked turns and swift drops, and Gram
Boos's ringlets dance and spring and she cackles
and pulls out my laughter. I hear her steady
release in the intervening decades when I draw
near a classic coaster or improbably find myself
in a car at the top of the ride.

A ROAD TO WELLNESS

At Clyde Hill Elementary the class lined
up to be weighed and measured and I
shuffled to the end if I could. One nurse
chanted numbers while a second wrote
longhand in a ledger. That voice terrified me

since I outweighed everyone. I ate well
and passed 100 pounds in third grade.
When the nurse announced my weight
red hot shame spread beyond my cheeks,
through my clothes. I slunk off fearing

a chorus of titters. In sixth grade,
following national personal fitness directives,
I heaved my head upward for sit-ups
but my stomach got in the way. In Boy
Scouts I sized up the Personal Fitness

merit badge, an obstacle to Eagle rank.
I ticked off requirements until
the seven chin-ups. In an after-school
gym room, no one present, I asked
Mr. Bourque to witness and sign off

a miracle. I'd practiced and hoped for
divine grace as I somehow rose and dropped
four times. Halfway to the pole on my fifth,
I stalled but wouldn't relent. I strained, turned
red then purple then swarthier than Mr.

Bourque who spoke as though from Boston.
I shuddered, he gleamed, said "stop, quit it, I'll
give ya credit." He wanted no burst vessels, I
wanted that badge. A half century later,
after decades of running, I remember chin

on bar and hear that coach's anxious voice,
crediting me with fitness I wouldn't fully
earn for years. I never played ball for him
but his generosity opened a path I jogged,
fierce devotee of wellness for the long run.

WELCOME TO COLLEGE

I awake to the buzzer, glasses off,
pull the dorm door open where the tall
rectangular trash can, carefully propped,

tips into me. My pajama bottoms wet,
crumbled paper balls float past my ankles,
white flotsam that bobs past heavier deposits

near feet. Back then, the buzzer hurried us
to the common phone at hall's end, but instead
of a beautiful co-ed's voice asking for me,

a thumbtack presses my room button.
I'm seventeen, recently shed of thirty-five
pounds but not conceit, my noxious body odor.

I take it personally: who would do this to *me*?
not as a generic prank, one of those welcome-
to-college-life gestures, no harm intended.

Maybe I belonged here as little as I did
in high school with its spotlit popular kids,
that predictably exclusive club I scorned, a non-member.

My rude baptism, not full immersion, turns up
my doubt about this place and my fit within it,
as though already relegated among those *Animal House*

rejects. It takes two months before my
suspicion dissipates, a low nimbus cloud
that drifts east and leaves clear air and a stone

path I walk, despite the slew of setbacks
and insecurities, into an academic future
called tenure-track. I never quit college:
still a promised land.

ANIMAL HOUSE

Big meatballs fly, explode on impact
against faces, walls, beams while
tendrils of cooked spinach trail,
airborne clusters, droop, spread
over hair, festoon beams. Some dive
under tables, others chew placidly

as food shatters on tables or clothes.
A hasher, I've served these unstable
isotopes, tonging them onto cafeteria
trays, a wet mound of spinach dropped
onto one of the tray's small squares.
Sylvia Jenkins, Jewett dining hall director,

inhales sharply, shakes her head as a few
stray balls arc behind the serving
line, splat against the stainless
steel refrigerators. One older worker
harrumphs. In a lull after the first
frenzy, I seize the day, hold one glob

aloft, loudly quaver, "Does anyone want
another meatball?" One of my best
performances in the segregated hall
where boys will be boys and where
the freshmen men skip three meals
to pay for cleanup. Did we pull this shit?

At reunions I ask, do you remember
the food fight? Why do we chuckle?
Why doesn't embarrassment curb
the wave of fond frivolity? When
I watch that *Animal House* recognition
scene, my lips stretch before hanging

strands of spinach and meatball shrapnel.

GIRLFRIEND

We've never had sex. I unbutton her shirt,
unhook her bra, and she surges, kisses cover
my face then she withdraws while we sit
on her rumpled sheets in semi-darkness,
my pants unzipped. Her confession leaks
over my body: "I had an abortion last month."

We'd walked together in London and I
drive hours to her cramped student apartment.
I could finally say "my girlfriend" with no
blush, stake a claim on her body as I had
her heart but her words pummel my stomach.
She says, "It was a mistake, just a quick

fling." Her eyes spill and she hugs me.
I zip my jeans and mumble. I return
to my college town and revise this draft—
contrary stories, contrary campuses—of my
life, one where we travelled together but then
did not and I tripped on my path.

MAHLER IN COLLEGE

Back in '72 I played Beethoven and Brahms
and Crosby Stills & Nash and Cat Stevens
albums in my dorm room, mixed it up
to mask my classical nerdiness. I showed
my stripes with Neil Young or James Taylor
but missed Led Zeppelin, too busy diving
into late Schubert chamber music or
anything by Ralph Vaughan Williams, whose
first name is pronounced Rafe, long a.

But an upperclassman next door, unassuming
appearance, greasy hair slicked along his
forehead, had me beat. On occasional Sunday
afternoons he'd put on Mahler's 3rd Symphony
which spanned two records and an hour
and a half. Gradually the dark trombone solo
in the long opening movement crept inside
my skin, the loud climax of the final movement
plunged deep, and I've never recovered.

INGMAR BERGMAN AND ME

In high school, your average moviegoer,
I watched *Black Orpheus* then *The Trial*
because of a smart teacher and my jaw
dropped. Marcel Camus' lithe, gyrating
bodies like Orson Welles' cigar smoke
and weird camera angles and focus
still dance inside me.

In college, in a small amphitheater
classroom, I saw Bergman's
The Seventh Seal: when Bengt Ekerot,
white-faced and black-cowled,
announces "I am Death" to Max von
Sydow on that dark beach,
I squirmed and forgot to breathe.

I'm not playing any chess game
but Bergman's and Mr. Death pops
in my head and then other black-
and-white frames from his early
60s triptych, Liv Ullmann's
freckled round face later: anguished
scenes in color spill over me.

The old wizard's language
pulls us into interior landscapes
I don't see well, though
I step ahead uncertainly.
Fierce northern sunlight shifts
shadows as I vainly seek human
figures or wild strawberries.

KRUMHORN

— for Kate Bracher

In the college consort I joined
the "buzzies," as close as I've
ventured to a double reed which

vibrates inside a wood cap:
the oboe's cruder parent.
Four bend forward clutching

our wooden Js, close in shallow
semi-circle, adjust breath pressure
until the chord or passing notes

fall into pitch, then we might
pause and smile. We formed
the Tielman Susato Krumhorn

Gesellschaft, named after a 16th-
century Flemish music publisher
whose Antwerp door read "At

the Sign of the Krumhorn" and whose
dances we piped on our "high"
(loud) winds. The TSKG wove

a banner and adopted a motto:
Cave ("Beware") *Krumhorn.* We blew
hard and our tonic buzz vibrated

beyond our ears into our small
audiences who grinned. When I
close my ears I hear the nasal
blat as reeds quiver and catch me.

A LONG WAY FROM HOME

I ride a local bus north from Tremadoc,
north *Cymru* and all passengers speak Welsh
whose rises and dips and the soft click
of the double "ll" engulf me. I've been
deepening my vowels to match British
phonetics, obscuring my American tongue
and traveling newly confident in the broad
country of spoken English. But in the front
passenger seat, backpack alongside,
I discover a country more foreign than
Español for the first time, and it rings
in my ears when I walk up the mountain
highway in dark December. I'm
farther from home than ever before:
a strange land that lures and teases.
I bank my fears and venture
out with tongue, ready to stumble
and pick myself up again and again.

HANDS ON

"Do you mind?" the young wife asks
as she flattens my palm and pulls
closer. "I've inherited full powers
from my aunt," she reassures.
She's served me tea in her small
B & B in Kyle of Lochalsh where I've
hitchhiked from Glasgow with a
Yorkshireman. I stare across the
narrow passage to Skye, hear
Mendelssohn's Hebrides Overture,
step along this Outer edge clotted
with islands and crofts and round
burial mounds and Gaelic curses.

The new country unfolds along
my right hand as the wife hunches,
her index finger pressing its three
primary creases, unparallel, and a
host of minor intersecting lines
flanged like Martian *canali* favored
by Percival Lowell. She releases her
tight grip: "You have a weak lifeline,"
she concludes. Her hand squeezes
mine reassuringly as she retreats
to her kitchen. She writes music,
sends her scores to Glasgow's
Conservatory. She fingers my hand
like a cello's neck, a song in a
minor key. Since then I raise my
hand and squint, resist the verdict
on that square midland below my
broad fingers and thumb.

LONDON VIRGIN

When I exit the Arnos Grove tube stop after the concert, I pass several blokes with smokes leaning against a fence. They peg me foreigner. One steps forward, asks "How's your love life, mate?" then he spins and his right arm arcs and his fist smashes into my right eye. I don't have a love life. Shyness still streaks through me, steady current below my pompous noise.

He doesn't hit me again; his mates don't close with fists and feet. Just that one crack and blood seeps into my eye from the eyebrow cut. Quick whim, testosterone release. Random luck. I stagger through the park, wallet and ID intact, reach my homestay family's "semi-detached." Norma cleans the cut. I struggle to stretch the eye to pop out my contact lens.

On my twentieth birthday I am propositioned then slugged and the next day I stumble, not quite falling, trying to right myself, step forward on my own path. I swallow then gag that pair of unexpected presents, a bitter drink.

Earlier, at a Bach choral concert this friendly guy a row behind invites me to the empty seat so I can follow the score splayed across his lap. He is also an Allan, plays piano at a girls' school gym. I suppress laughter as his ardent eyes seek mine. Thin curls droop off the fringes of his gleaming bald pate. You've seen him too.

When I return home next day, I find a series of phone messages increasingly frequent. Call back call back. Let's get together. I blush, my stomach squirts acid as his desire undresses my naivete. An innocent abroad, I miss the gaydar on this date, later avoid the phone. My body's antennae extend as I picture for years the older Allan, two l's, who never closes with the younger. Poor bastards. I forgive us both.

Manny has taken me to the hospital clinic and I wait in the queue as my wannabe lover keeps ringing the flat. We wait longer in an airless hall. Next day I emerge in class, Alice Cooper makeup, and bask in the brief light of popularity. The light fades fast.

I've grown another pair of eyes on the sides of my head. I walk the streets of London and my future. I watch my back. Maybe I know a smidgen more about the body's desire. When I close my eyes, I still hear the smack of fist in eye socket, the frantic summons of a phone. Happy Birthday, mate. I shed a skin.

LINES COMPOSED LONG AFTER WORDSWORTH

A response to "Lines Composed a Few Miles above Tintern Abbey,
On Revisiting the Banks of the Wye during a Tour. July 13, 1798"

From Chepstow Castle I walk the lower valley
of the Wye past squared green fields
and trim cottages to the grassy flat where
Wordsworth's famed poem looms alongside
the roofless Abbey church and figure
and ground freeze into countless paintings.
On this silent sabbath I strain to hear
"The still sad music of humanity" in
the river's low murmur. How can I avoid
the poet's presence amidst these composed
ruins? Do his slow ruminative lines obscure
the picturesque composition? Place lives
before and after poem which addresses,
after all, the valley, not this site. No one
disturbs my communion with Gothic
lights and bare deciduous ridges beyond:
gnarled background to steep gray stone.

I step over the low fence—two hours
until winter opening time—and wander
the aisles and scan details while
guilt fogs my "elevated thoughts" of poet
and place. I walk upriver miles, pass
Wordsworth's spot, interrupted
only by a stray car, fishermen under
green umbrellas. I hitchhike to old Monmouth,
home of Henry V, and four jolly girls
ride me through two villages to a cold youth

hostel in the Forest of Dean where, before
the gas fire, my feet remember the day
and I renew my membership in wandering
William's party, "well pleased to recognize
/ In nature and the language of the sense
/ The anchor of my purest thoughts."

"TUCK IN, LAD!"

I hesitate before a heaped plate
at the table opposite Mr. Jack Tudor
whose waistcoat proclaims his paunch
and who instructs, "tuck in, lad"

and, at twenty, I do. His watch chain sparkles
in soft light and he balances peas
on his knife. Jack and Hilda, shirttail
relatives, open their south Wales

home to this wandering youth.
I'd buy my meats from his family
business. After I've digested
breakfast bacon, I'm sent on my

way with eight meat sandwiches
and a pound. Years later Mom, eager cook
and server, adopted Jack's command
which carried a note of mockery

since, utensils clutched, we always
set to. Dad said we ate "with a coming
appetite," savored the phrase. He felt
"peckish." Now when I am slow at table,

mimicking my wife's ruminative tempo,
I hear Mom's voice overlay Jack's
and my stomach remembers
though a less hearty trencherman.

STEP-GRANDMOTHER

Gram Barb serves her bland meatloaf then declares at table,
"Why, this is the best meatloaf I've tasted in a long while!"
She stirs the hot chocolate sauce in a small saucepan,
spoon steady rhythm, and later it trickles down the
dish's vanilla mound, cools, and the bite melts on tongue.
I still taste it.

She chews each bite a dozen times before she swallows
and I mask my yawns, my plate long empty.
She sits slightly forward in the wingback chair, knees
rub, legs parallel, the skirt hem well below knees.
She purrs, "mmnnn-hmnnn," a fat cat bright for
tidbits of conversation, and chirps "Oh, for pity's sake!"

She drives her '65 Plymouth Barracuda, sleek yellow
paint against black interior, to market Saturday mornings,
5,000 miles after 20 years.
At the beach, in baggy capri jeans, she walks slowly,
head bent over the outgoing tide's freshly-washed
stones, in search of agates.

She borrowed a Chinese drum from the Deacons
and never returned it. When asked, she'd fetch it
from the front closet, saying,"I like to play it." She beat
the drum for half a minute, smile pasted on her face.

She stocks canned food in basement cupboards for decades
including over 100 cans of tuna. A few bulge and gleam.
"You never know," she says.
She stockpiles newspapers and magazines and tools
in the basement and the piles tilt, defying gravity.
The leftovers in the refrigerator wrinkle and sag,

green with mold, and she says, "I can't remember when I opened that" or "I'm going to finish that tonight."

Then we had to take her away.

HOLD ME

Alec, four, capers as we enter
the old folks home, find our
way to my step-grandmother's
semi-private room where he

bounces while the roommate
gestures for me to clutch then
empty her piss bag. I soothe
feeble Gram Barb with

platitudes she drinks as Alec,
bright smile, stretches the dull
room beyond its flimsy privacy
curtains. After his quick hug

we retreat to the lobby,
walkers and wheelchairs
in random assortment
that occasionally shift as do

limbs, jaws, or eyes. When Alec
passes out of my grasp, eyes
draw close, moths to small
flame, and desire reaches stilled

arms as though hands touch
his warm skin and active limbs.
They yearn to hug him and remember
the surge of skin on skin.

ON BECOMING A PROFESSOR

By sixth grade, tongue busy, I decided to become
a teacher; by freshman year in college, I took aim
at the life led by my professors.

My career as a tubist reached its peak and after
quitting those low brass sonorities, I seemed
to belch more, which worried father, as did my

decision to major in English. Endowed with a mighty
wind and a barrel of obstinacy, I blew other notes
through grad school and launched my career, despite

a sagging job market, at a private college where I
confirmed my love of my voice. Since then, I've shaded
my earnestness, an unneeded necktie, and tuned my ears

to students' stories even as I play a few of mine like
this one. The calling still fits though I wear humble
clothes, ever more certain of what I don't know.

GO EAST, YOUNG MAN

At the Seattle bus station I hug my parents
step up and turn left, sidle down the dim
aisle into my future. The drivers change
every eight hours but I remain. The seat's
soft pattern presses upon thighs, back,
and butt. I squirm, muscles tire from

inaction and sleep flits beyond my window
seat. I'm drugged, lulled, an adult toddler
in carrier seat on a ride towards morning
sun that never ends. When a new driver
climbs aboard, he slides his name plate
into the slot between three metal words

in block letters: SAFE, RELIABLE, COURTEOUS.
In Spokane a jolly black man sits close, talks
through the night about his friend in
"Mizzoola." His belly bulges my way on left
turns and his cheap wine breath hovers
over the acrid scent of urine.

East of Billings the driver announces,
"Now folks, sometimes on this section we
brake suddenly due to stock on the road."
A giant plastic cow near Bismarck
moos first light. When we reach Chicago
the bus spirals down a driveway below

the streets and I know I'm lost. Days
later another bus drops me in Amherst,
Virginia where, in four hours, another
will carry me the final miles to my new

life. Impatience flares and I walk
to the highway shoulder, thumb out.

This image of a far younger self slides
back into view at odd moments and I shudder
before the wash of disbelief. What was I
doing? Self-confidence, a thin mix,
shone like cheap veneer over thick ignorance.
I watch myself as I stand forever at that

crossroads as August's humid heat white-
washes oak forests, blurs pastures and low
hills: I wear gray polyester slacks because I don't
know any better, underpants and shirt sweat
wet, and clutch an umbrella and portable Smith-
Corona typewriter case, promise of my new self.

I am twenty-one in a new time zone,
thousands of miles east of my past, dozens
of miles south of the near-future, suspended
in hot wet air new to my body. I smell
myself and anxiety like shyness, a constant
companion, prickles my skin, stranger in a

strange land. But stubbornness, older
kin than shyness, keeps my right thumb
cocked and soon a car slows before my
"honest face" as a British driver once said.
I ride into my new town with an old
university designed by Thomas Jefferson

which had finally begun admitting women
and even a Northwesterner. I gather gear,
clutch a map, ride a taxi whose vowels
swim past my ears. I breathe deeply, slip
into that new skin called graduate student.

MAN WITH MOP

Grad school on pause, broke back home
I wring the mop in the bucket then swab
the hall in tight figure eights. Third shift at a local
community college where, Masters in hand,

I should teach. I empty waste baskets, push
the vacuum in a classroom and at the front
desk I box anger, release the white-collar
daytime bubble, head down until the 2:30 a.m.

lunch break. One guy holds a Masters in art
history but we never talk. Around 4:00 a.m.,
skunk hour, I remove used tampons
in the women's bathroom, wipe down surfaces,

scan for anything out of place, and I
dream those long reading lists trailing
each grad class like kite tails, my return
months and miles ahead, wait shift's end.

I drive home as dawn edges the Cascades'
silhouette, toss and turn until Noon
and my fingers still grip the mop's handle,
out of joint with daylight's world and myself.

TEACHER EVALUATION

I wave my hands, aim for eloquence,
my back to the tree trunk, the upper-
level class camped about me, when
the passing bird shits on my tan pants.
No student receives the baptism and I
pause, focused upon early Neruda,
announce "I've been shat upon,"
eager to use the old past tense.
I point to the white blotch mid-thigh
and students chuckle. I say,
"After all these years, the most
succinct comment on my pedagogy
I've ever seen!" During the break I
rush to the Provost, old friend, eager
to show and tell. This mundane
lesson, gravity's surprise, punctures
my persona.

SEAWEED LOVE

On a summer afternoon, the tide creeps over hot sand,
an expanding sheet of glass before a north wind ruffles
the surface, and both sons stride in beyond their knees.
Their eyes search small clumps of seaweed that cluster
and drift at tide's whim. I crouch farther out, skin adjusted
to salt water's chill challenge. For a short time I am still

taller, offer a broader target as they seize slimy wads
and fling them at me, then one another. I duck their
overhead or sidearm pitches, maneuver and return
volleys, but a loud smack on my back or chest prompts
their hoots and redoubles their aim. I blink, wear their
suits as I throw seaweed bombs with my brothers

at our father who paddles and blows like an old turtle,
his suit bulging with air pockets. In old age with ALS
he quit the beach, and years after death we scatter his
ashes here on a high tide. I shake my head, throw
again, picture myself tipping to old age where I back-
stroke alone, sons scattered into their adult geographies.

My body imagines the wet slap, a tendril code through
which fathers and sons touch.

TUMBLING WITH SONS

When they were toddlers
almost a decade apart, both sons
waited to "wrestle" with me.
I lay on the floor,
they crawled over me,
and I extended my legs or arms
or tossed them up until I
couldn't and we kneeled
and bumped and I rode them
around the room, bucked
and jerked, and they hooted
and giggled. And asked
for more until they trudged
off to "play adventures."
Soon enough in their
lengthening, they no longer
asked and sometimes I
remember our entwined
bodies, their hot skin
on mine, and I know
this is as good as it gets.

"EVERYTHING WILL BE ALRIGHT"

Mid-afternoon the day Mother dies,
my brothers and I retreat to the waiting
area as the nurse hooks up her Dilaudid
drip. After nineteen days she fades faster
and our numb bodies creep over the hours.
I pound the big window's metal frame,
yell "Goddammit!" My older brother
reaches out with his right arm, clasps
my shoulders.

He wears words like "aloof," "withdrawn,"
has never moved out on his own, never
touches unless returning my handshake.
Only his eyes or rare guffaws bridge
the cool space around him.

My younger brother reassures Mother
each day, "Everything will be alright;
"we'll take care of everything," even
her oldest son, the bright laser of
anxiety in her old age. We carry her
burden, a worm in the gut. Later
we give our brother over one year
to pack up, move on, but he drags
his days.

Our last night together he barely speaks,
and after his forced move he erects
tall walls, closes contact. In the loud
lengthening silence, a second death.
My shoulders imagine his warm hand again.

"I WOULD PREFER NOT TO"

In my aging, having taught
Melville's inscrutable *Bartleby*
over the decades, I like to think
I've penetrated behind the screen
beyond those stray crumbs,
stacks of ledgers and papers
in want of copying.
I like to think I know more
than his puzzled employer
in his airless chamber
on Wall Street so when
Bartleby parts his lips
and quietly chants his
credo, that polite "no"
loud like thunder, I
hover nearby and nod
in silent agreement.

ELBERTA '13

I pop the lid of that last jar
of Elberta peaches, canned
by Mother the year before she
died. At ninety she still
peels and halves, stands over
the boiler as steam wets her
wrinkled cheeks. She's canned
for generations and our tongues
know what her pears, peaches,
apricots should taste like.

In the store I toss my head
at fruit in cans. My belly
discriminates. As my spoon slices
small sections of the last Elberta,
a variety Mom favored, I slide
the peach piece around my tongue
and Mom appears, boss in her small
kitchen, assured as she tongs lids
in place, awaits the tonk that seals
her labor.

TREE = TRUTH

"Never let anyone touch this tree," a local arborist
        told my mother decades ago.
Dad planted the redwood in the '60s before
        the remodel and it rose,
a widening cone with fat base, near
        the new garage's front corner.
I trimmed lowest branches, swept needles
        every visit, fingered red
tan bark, deeply cracked and seamed; burnished ridges
        slid under my fingers.
Stepping away, I'd lean far back, follow
        the tapering cone to its
peak, confident in its aspirations beyond
        the second-growth Doug firs
which danced in the wind before my child eyes.

Years after the sale, no sign of habitation,
        only my puzzled shrugs; moss
bunches across the lower patio, ivy crawls
        up the brick fireplace,
spirea and azalea and rhododendron branches careen
        and sag like burst fireworks.
Dad's apple trees, unpruned and unharvested,
        grow into each other,
a spindly web, and gray scale and moss
        creep on the trunks while
the house settles behind its white gray paint
        like Miss Havisham's wedding
dress. Worse than any teardown or makeover,
        this blight rots
our generations of care, mocks our husbandry,

my parents' years of planting, my years of fertilizing
            and weeding and trimming.
Our shrubs zoom unchecked, indifferent to absent
            owners who ignore
the old story except for the most valuable tree:
            a far north green candle,
Sequoia sempervirens. They pay loggers who fell
            it and nearby firs
whose rounds settle in ivy, a jumble of giant
            discs quietly decomposing,
unused like the house. My rage churns my stomach.
            I struggle
to inhabit a mind that destroys tree truth,
            that reduces tall life
to cast off clumps beyond hands or heart,

to "the slow smokeless burning of decay."

CARRY ME BACK

The oaks and hickories flame
in morning and afternoon light,
fling autumnal oranges, dull
browns, piercing reds, the show
not over in early November.

Can I seize this younger self,
blond hair and unwrinkled face,
from another life in a distant state
whose hardwood ridges and
undulating pastures tear my heart again?

My eyes hurt in this drenched
pastoral I forgot though feet
remember the Blue Ridge's rising
then falling tide and skin beads
from the press of humid air.

In this upper Piedmont I stalk
a graduate student and young
husband who strides just ahead
and out of reach, intent on books,
papers, courses, a wife soured

by competition, and indifferent
faculty who smoke in class. I
pretend to touch that man dogged
in his program, nobody's favorite,
resolved to finish, find an academic

career. Who is that out-of-place
figure moist from wet air
who pushes past Jefferson's
white pillars, graduates with a
degree in inferiority, learns

the game at a Blue Ridge college,
whose marriage sags then dies?
He eludes me in the way earlier
selves disappear in mist. But in
the mirror, if I peer long enough,

a ghost flashes.

DÉJÀ VU

Long after the sale, we stop in Clyde Hill,
park across the street, steeled for change.
An uninhabited ranch style obscured
behind a laurustinus hedge and apple trees
and shrubbery, from which I launched east,
farther and farther, four decades ago.

A migratory bird, I flew back many seasons
through unfixed days. But aging parents then
deaths, an old plot, forced sale and farewell to
the house of my past. I picture cut Douglas
firs, uprooted rhodys, the dump pile signs
of renovation for strangers. Instead, our surname

shines, affixed below the sturdy mailbox stand
Dad built, and just past the laurustinus my wife
notes the small azalea, orange-red blossoms, we
bought and planted for Mom. In the breezeway
the same begonia box below the window.
Two pieces of driftwood carried back from our

saltwater beach cabin. Unpicked apples line
the curving driveway, rot in soft turf. No one
has pruned fruit trees or vine maple or shrubs,
my shears gone. In the backyard, neglect piles up,
fir branches ungathered. All plants in place,
their stretching shapes accuse me, chief gardener

and maintenance man the past score of years.
The rec room's oval braided rug visible again
after thirty years under the live-at-home brother's
careless boxes of CDs and DVDs, his slop.

At the breezeway window, I study the dining room's
blue-green slate, the small breakfast bar over

which peers my mother's small portable TV.
In the living room my father's stained pine lattice
shelves, bereft of books and sculpture. Only three
folding chairs on our mustard carpet hint at any
strangers. I raise my head, watch Mother shuffle
down the hallway with her walker, chin raised,

her passage quiet—she's almost there. All signs
point to my family, our vacancy and disappearance
only an illusion. A deserted house dormant for several
seasons, still ours, as though waiting this bird's return.
A silent reproach to sale and infidelity, it mutely awaits
a new command, some promise of inhabitation. I walk away

flooded by guilt, past crowding out present, chastened
by the soft October sunlight, knowing in my bones you
can't go home again yet knowing that home, wherever
it gathers like a braid of fond scents, arose just here,
in this very ground where a family stuck for sixty years
then drew away, called by death and other loves.

Section III.

OBSERVATIONS AND PROFESSIONS

CLOSER

This winter's plunging cold pulls the mountains
and ridgelines closer, particularly before sunset
when yellow-pink alpenglow washes the peaks
so that they draw near and gleam unlike any

other season, nod to me and each other.
Distances close when the full moon, fat platter,
lights our valley and shines like a lamp,
mornings, reluctant to droop out of sight.

Below zero the high borders beyond sagebrush
pull in, each rock face or meadow a snow-
white patch, each line of lodgepoles etched
as though it all huddles like me, reaches its core.

PROCESSION

Sometime in April mustard crocuses push
out, fan inside their splayed leaves, end
winter's subdued dun palette, opening

act to Wordsworth's daffodils, cream
or yellow, bunched and sturdy against
final frosts at dawn. As they fade

pink-white tulips and a stray red
rise higher, their rounding petals cup
warming sun. Then the flowering

almond tree pinks the far garden,
the delicate blossoms wave in
tight clusters. They droop before

Whitman's lilacs in the thick hedge
close by whose packed spiral cones
arrow and spill, scent the yard.

After their lavender dulls, the seven
Harison's rosebushes along the
sidewalk explode, a riot of pioneer

yellow like frozen Roman candles
at the top of their radial burst that
light the yard at dusk. Then

the Oriental poppies like hooded
cobras stretch and nod, open
their broad orange faces all over

the place and it's "rainbow, rainbow, rainbow everywhere" and I bow my head in gratitude, my eyes blurred.

HANDS ON STONE

Atop the Dillon Overlook Trail
a low rock arch squats upon
the sparse hilltop for seasons.
A rough "C" tilted ahead 90
degrees, firmly footed, it offsets
the valley panorama beyond.
What hands shaped the arch,
set the keystone pieces just so
to best gravity, shale flakes
framing the hole of air?

What hands knocked it down?
Did they push against the arch,
upset the balance out of a child's
irresistible whim? Did a teenager's
shoe kick one side like a soccer
ball, a vandal's glee unattached
to any motive, only the blunt blow?

What hands gathered flat leaves,
layered and tested every set,
patiently built a round cairn
a yard thick and taller than me
with conical top? Worthy of
shepherds a century ago
with extra time who loved
to handle shale, build a child's
tower that outlasted their
flocks and lives.

I pass with our Aussie shepherd
over cycles of months, trace

Shiva's contrary rhythms
of creation and destruction.
I palm this stout, smooth-sided
column, lean against its mass
no wind could topple; my flat
hands pat its top. How long
will the monument mark
the bald hill that opens
the valley yet pulls eyes
and fingers back to its assured
curves? Rock art rises
from the gentle work
of hands in a breeze:
the heart that stacks stone
outlasts the rude limbs
that aid gravity, tear down.

PASTURE PLAY

Peaked tents cluster in composed groups
in Stan's pasture along the river as I double
take. For years I jog past, greet two horses,
sole occupants, near their water trough

as they eye my dog and me, passing curiosity.
Now I struggle to take in this magic canvas,
a few kids running past the green honey
buckets, a man in doublet conversing

with three women who sport long gowns
only lacking tippet and ruff. The entrance
sign reads "SCA enter here," and I flash
back to college Renaissance Fairs as I

stretch my legs in tights, play recorder
or krumhorn, sway the pavan or hop
the volta, kick the circle branles or
the branle gay, our sinuous line weaving

between spectators, right legs raised
and poised for the next measure. In this
encampment a large archery target tilts
towards the road, but I see no central

green for broadax battle or dance, no
long banquet board on trestles. Not
Breughel's *Kermess*, but when I run
back, that man greets me and I say,

"I'm happy to see you here" and he
says, "Come on in and join the fun"
and I almost do because Stan's pasture
has never looked so gay.

Note: "SCA" is the Society for Creative Anachronism

KALEIDOSCOPE

One afternoon at the last century's end
a group of South African schoolteachers,
part of a Fulbright exchange, sit on wooden
benches in a loose circle in our white Montana
town then rise and break into song.

Their turbans and flowing dresses explode
in bright patterns as they chant and clap
and bend and swirl, a sinuous circle
in effortless dip and flow, and no one
has ever seen anything like that here.

I still see and hear their easy synchrony,
a fluid rhythm from childhood that taps
my envy, chastises my stiff limbs.

BEFORE BRUCE'S GRAVE

— for Amy

At Indian Creek Cemetery a round oak shades Bruce's grave
decked with an artificial bouquet, the headstone engraved
with Masonic and volunteer fireman's icons, and on the back-
side his favorite phrase, "Endeavor to Persevere."

Before it stands his big daughter, immobile in grief, as our tall
younger son draws close on her right and she curls her arm
across his lower back. Our short daughter falls into place
on the left, her arm crosses his daughter's lower back.

Three kin, contrary shapes, arms symmetric in their quiet embrace,
cheeks wet, mute before loss as the late afternoon sun dapples
the sward and Bruce's voice rumbles through us and I retreat
to the car, still angry at the hard bargain between Mr. Death and him.

MOTHER AND DAUGHTER

— for Lynn

Lynn stands behind the podium
behind the just closed casket draped
with flowers and a handmade quilt.
Her mother, stilled by Alzheimers, always
dressed well and wears a formal pink dress.

Lynn arranges her thick hair in easy waves
that frame her face. She wears matching
black and addresses the congregation
in this country Baptist church where her
parents and sister were married and her father

was buried in his early forties. Her voice
calmly measures her phrases and she
quickly regains control after sorrow surges
twice. Her mother's decades as widow
stretched out and covered her solitude.

My wife closes with Louise's advice,
and her alto enfolds her mother's high pitch
and dipthonged vowels: "Keep your seams
straight and your thimble on. Always have
something green on your plate. Never date

a Catholic: you might want to marry one.
Never serve the same food twice in one
meal. When you're buying a ham, always
get a butt. Stand straight and look 'em
in the eye," which Lynn models now,

and in her aging, her mother peeks out
of her body in her posture, the set of her
legs, her face in daydreams or pleasure
in blouses with bright embroidered patterns.
Though mother rests in death and daughter,

animated, stands straight, an unbroken
fabric threads between generations like one
of Louise's quilts both worked on whose
pattern delights the eye and whose weight
warms the body fortunate enough to recline

beneath it. Needles busy, both still stitch
towards one another. I hear two voices.

CORNUCOPIA

— in memory of Carol Templeton

Carol says "I'll just have a snack ready"
or "I'll fix breakfast for y'all" but we
know what this means. In addition
to yeast rolls and marinated pork
tenderloin in strips and cheese grits
and an egg-and-ham quiche whose
crust might float away unless anchored,
she fries bacon and country sausage
and scrambles eggs with half a stick
of butter. Fresh cut fruit mounds
and glistens in a bowl and we haven't
reached the walnut-apple bunt cake
with caramel frosting or the second
bunt cooked with sweet blackberry
wine or the berry cobbler in a round
pie dish whose crust thickens with
melted chocolate. Desserts require
their own staging area.

As my eyes eat everything before
tongue tastes, laughter bubbles up
before the challenge. For my mother-
in-law's funeral, Carol bakes a strawberry
cake eight inches high, a thick field
of sweet white roses amidst chocolate-
covered strawberries, dark round
boulders, atop. Big and jolly, as
though prerequisite, a sculptor
with sugar and eggs and butter
and baking pans, Carol cooks

for dozens when we visit and sends
us off with filled tupperwares, plastic
forks, paper plates. She giggles over
my profuse compliments, my forays
through desserts we never eat or I
never see. When we hug she says,
like many Southerners, "Y'all come
back now!" And we do, after seasons
and the return of our usual waistlines.

STUCK SHIFT

A couple quick errands downtown
then I turn onto S. Atlantic in my
'86 Mazda B-2000 underpowered
but dependable, yet when I shift
to second there's no clutch, my left
foot gropes for the pedal that's stuck,
my heart sticks my breath quickens,
and in the mid-morning sunlight
I ride in a new world like a fast
trip inside Wonderland and I
putt south down the main drag,
shift smoothly to third and maybe
fourth but keep speed down,
signal left swing into my auto
mechanic's, pull into neutral,
engine steady though I'm not
but my left hand pries, springs
the frozen pedal back to its
customary position left
of the matching brake pedal,
yet I don't bounce back for
awhile, instead ponder the
recurrence of stuck shift.

YOUNG MOTHER

The young Crow woman eases into a chair, joins a small group in the white class, tells me "My son is two months old, but I want to continue my education." A father of three, I melt. She nurses him and when problems arise, she flies to him. She says, "The father is back home on the rez." I tell her, "I sympathize. I want you to succeed, but you have the same work as everyone." My kneejerk fairness standard bores me. She comes when she can but sits silent, listens even when we discuss Sarah Winnemucca or Zitkala-Sa. Is her quiet her respect?

When I ask, she says, "It's interesting to hear what others think." Her papers show a recent voice who anchors herself, now and then, in standard American English. She arrives late, leaves early, misses and I, helpless, want to change the plot, surprise us both, close the gap between past and this academic present, a bright light. But she fails and part of me protests this pre-scripted tragedy. I fail too.

ON PLAYING SCHUBERT SONATAS

For a quarter century I ignored the mute glances
of our old upright, walnut veneer, which my wife
and I restored before our marriage. Now

I fold open the ivory keyboard my fingers
have known since childhood and they find
their way again inside *The Complete Sonatas*

for Pianoforte Solo, the red-covered Dover
edition whose cover features an oval
reproduction of an engraving of an 1820s

musicale, friends crowding Schubert, slightly
bent, playing a spinet piano. I read through
movements, try fingerings, repeat tough

passages, my tempi slower than marked.
I play again, the moods of each movement
opening out, here the development,

here the recapitulation, and Schubert's
harmonic world washes over me. Some themes
sing and I sigh, eyes wet, and remember

Stravinsky's rebuttal when someone said
Schubert's long works put the listener
to sleep: no "matter because when he woke

up, he was in paradise" and I am, every
time. No soporific, rather an elixir and I
vibrate long after the strings stop.

BUSHRA ARRIVES IN BOISE

After hours above 30,000 feet,
more time zones, Bushra
and her children stumble
down corridors through passport
control under the florescent
din. Eyes blink, hearts
flutter at the welcoming gate.

Bushra clutches the sheaf
of fresh flowers swaddled
in cellophane; her white head-
scarf edges her forehead
and cheeks, offsets coffee skin.

Bushra waits and waits
before the gate, frozen before
the doors to her new life
in a dry land.

> *Based on a photograph and caption in "The Lucky Ones," a photography
> exhibit in the University of Montana Western Art Gallery, Dillon,
> Montana, a few years ago. According to the caption, Bushra took
> almost an hour to pass beyond the welcoming gate.*

MADONNA AT THE BOTTOM OF
THE STAIRWELL

Now my matted framed poster
of Munch's *Madonna* hangs
at the bottom of our stairs.
She used to reign over rows
of office bookshelves, but we
moved her and she marks
my daily descents from bedroom
and office.

I've seen lots of Madonnas
painted in earlier centuries
and Munch's Virgin Mary ain't
no virgin. Eyes closed in ecstasy,
her head tilts slightly back,
right arm languidly extended
behind her, elbow crooked,
fresh from sex:

a vermilion halo frames her
disheveled black hair that frames
her face—dark eye sockets, pointy
nose, closed cupid lips—and neck,
and tresses splay across her left
shoulder, curl around her left
breast, taut and rounded like
her right breast with its red
nipple that matches her red navel:

breasts lift slightly outward
from each other. She's full
of the Holy Spirit. Now when I

drop the nine steps, she embraces
me as I stand face to face
and disappear in the soft space
between her breasts: there's
world enough and time. I've
got the spirit too and the day smiles.

"MAKE AMERICA GREAT AGAIN"

Whose America?
I know, before sexual minorities, before hyphenated Americans,
before "aliens" and illegals, before fuckin' Woke cancel culture
(oh by the way when did your people arrive?);
those shining good ol' days when white men called the shots
when business was supreme, undisputed;

when manufacturing jobs and factory shifts supported families,
when unions counted for something and we watched football
and Detroit and DC politicians actually talked to one another,
before "outsource" became a verb that closed plants
and made millionaires much fatter inside the top 1-percent fortress.

Whose America?
I know, when we kicked ass whenever and wherever we wanted
on the globe, when women stayed home or at least stayed in place
and no woman would ever think she'd be Commander-in-Chief
because—well, you know, a woman over our military?
You gotta be kidding. When gas and burgers were cheap

and our paycheck spread much further, but for decades we fall
further behind, traffic sucks, we're pissed so let's blame
all these new groups dancing in media spotlights, or darker-
skinned immigrants. Our America felt simpler, less hot,
less crowded, and we want it back. We tweet. Now.

11/9

Most days I bank my anger as though
a volcano plugs its vents, a perfect explosion
of age, career, and national elections. Why do
I, aging academic, bob beyond the red margins,
count for nothing, find no place at the table?

How does democracy sing 9/11 then 11/9,
code for eruption of a new internal kind,
less palpable for legions of mad voters who
cheer, mouths wet, the billionaire who blasts
and tweets and appoints the wealthiest Cabinet

in history, foxes who guard respective henhouses
turned magma chambers? Rage erupts like thick
pyroclastic blasts and I will my dormancy, turn
away from my American shame, a hot flow, lost
in the gap between what we've been and what

we are which stretches out of sight. I pick up
cinders of *citizen*, uncertain how to re-glue
as Humpty Dumpty, certain that many hate
"eggheads." That ol' "wisdom of the common man"
myth bursts beyond other claims. The anger

and blare of the Prez trump my own
and with the bellow of kneejerk exceptionalism—
rising pressure with gauge needles ticking
beyond vertical—something's gotta give.

TWEETSTER

Tweet
Tweet tweet
tweet   tweet tweet tweet
tweet   TWEET!!
!!!
re-tweet   re-tweet!

No Tweetie Bird no twittersation
no birdsong only flipping the bird,
only his busy thumbs as
his simian lips curl, purse, uncurl

THE WISDOM OF THE COMMON MAN

Democracy is the theory that the common people know what
they want, and deserve to get it good and hard.
                                                    —H. L. Mencken

I live in Wisconsin between Madison and Milwaukee
but stay away from both especially Madison, that
liberal bastion of jackoffs who don't put in a day's work,
good thing Governor Walker dumped public employees'
bargaining rights, now if he could only end tenure
which might jerk those eggheads off their asses.
Fuckin' know-it-alls. My chin sags like my thighs
in my barcalounger. I've worked in the same shop
since high school graduation and though it's not closing
soon, the money just doesn't cover everything anymore
even with the wife's shift. My union membership drops
a little, the local always voted Dem but hey, that rich bitch
in New York don't care about us. She thinks she can get
away with anything. She's no Commander-in-Chief. What
a joke! I'm going with the guy who'll MAKE AMERICA
GREAT AGAIN. I toss my old PBR at the screen when
O'Reilly mentions Obama. Remember about Obama
and Osama? Only one letter difference. Come on!
I reload from my Igloo, toast Donald T., the guy who
will take care of business. True, my belly bulges against
my '86 Lynryd Skynyrd T-shirt, looks like I'm wearing
an inner tube. Got to cut down on the fried cheese and
Doritos, eat better, turn Fox off, take a walk--something.
Maybe my anger will subside like my belly should. I
voted for the winner, never mind the screwy vote, and let
those stuck-up bastards in Madison or anywhere
eat it. Good and hard.

PATRIOTISM

On Superbowl Sunday
    I walk the dog
        in the hills
            west of town,

return to the new
    Thoreau biography
        I'm halfway through:
            now he's published

"On Civil Disobedience,"
    that majority of one,
        and I'm a Patriot
            too just like Henry.

WHITE HEAT

Tiki torches flicker as 300 men, sweat
beading on GI Joe haircuts, yell "Blood
and Soil!" "Whose streets? Our streets!"
as they swagger north along the University
of Virginia's lawns past ducking students,
swirl beyond Jefferson's Rotunda,
circle his statue,
chant "Jews will not replace us,"
press outnumbered counter-protesters,
stab Dean Groves who bleeds
rescuing pepper-sprayed students.

Wrong aim.

First Amendment protection of this hate
crime? Administration and police asleep
at the wheel that night and following
day? This rape scene only lacks pointy
white hoods and a lynching rope.
Images of *Kristalnacht* and book burnings
and random arrests flash before me as
the brownshirts go after *Die Juden*
whom Goebbels proclaims "vermin."
These marchers dribble anti-Semitic
boilerplate, unaware of its meanings,
its long dark trail. They know just
enough to toss the flare of these phrases
aloft with their guttering torches. How
do we rub out gleaming white faces
and beards overrunning my university?
How do I fold up my outrage about
skinheads on the prowl who shake

their torches at Jefferson who stands
an impossible distance apart?

The Grounds, where I return and walk
with family short months later, echoes
with the chants of racists who trod
unchallenged, whose desecration
burns my eyes.

Charlottesville, Virginia, 8/11/2017

DISPLACEMENT

In the hotel lobby
Ziyad, 23, stands before
the American group
including students his age,
his black hair curled
flat above his coffee
face as his eyes flit
and he shifts under
the weight of our gaze,
the introduction by Yorgos,
tour company owner
and Ziyad's sponsor.

The President announces
troop withdrawal, walking
away from Kurdish allies
caught between Turks and Assad,
Syrians in their home ground.
In Athens we meet a Kurd
who stumbles in English,
his third or fourth language.

Ziyad lives in a refugee
camp hours west, reaches
the big city irregularly.
He knows nothing about
parents or siblings. His
town has been bombed.

The other professor and I
try and put Ziyad at ease,
engage him but he volunteers

little. Students try to scroll
backwards in Ziyad's life,
fail.

He joins us on the bus,
sits at the table with Yorgos
and other Greeks, away
from our carafes and laughter
and live music and stage for
dancing. His strained face
the poster of international
refugees who, unsettled,
unsettle us at home
and abroad. Home in flames,
his darker skin accuses
our complacency and privilege
in Island America. His face
pops before me, pricks
my skin.

SOCIAL DISTANCE

Who would have thought?
Wide space too far away
to nod heads together, easy
over coffee beer or food,
or to touch or make love:
buzz phrase, unplanned currency
and oxymoron that governs
our new norm, safe distance
beyond coughs or sneezes
but removed from one
another, reduced to smart phones
and computers that promise
we're a part rather than apart;

If we're social creatures
though some aren't, we live
against our grain when we
huddle at home away from
face-to-face in class or office
or store or brewery or café
or city park or campfire
or choir room. Is 6 feet enough?
Should it be 12 feet? "Social distance"
strains against itself, hygienic
safe zone wars against our nature,
constrains our movements,
demands we damp down desire
because getting together might
sicken or kill us though staying
put taxes our hearts so we seek
other colors in our same gray days.

A POEM FROM THE PLAGUE YEAR

Eight months into the pandemic
a gray rat scurries into the garage through
the fat gap below the door.

The rat wriggles in and out
a new home
and I distribute turquoise

poison pellets inside, remember
Kafka's cockroach and giant mole
when I track the rat's sturdy tail.

No rat has moved in since.

The rat hustles like a bad dream,
eats the poison,
leaves no trace.

CORONAVIRUS ARIA

In Italia in the evening
instead of *passeggiata*
folks gather on their balconies
lean out and lift their voices
sing "Il Canto degli Italiani"
in harmony or rise
with a pop tune or beat
their improved drum kits,
flare spatulas on pot lids.

Hospitals clot with patients
who force tough choices
on drooping physicians while
cemetery and crematoria staff
work overtime. Too many bodies,
bleak bubonic echo.

Instead of telling stories
like Boccaccio's affluent youngsters
who quit Firenze to repose
in the quiet countryside
dotted with olive groves,
apartment dwellers step out,
apart but a part as they
erupt in song and rhythm
for each other, a cacophonous
"Va, pensiero" against the new
black death. Their voices float
and knit in the night air,
defy the virus.

ONE VOICE

I sit near my mother-in-law as we watch
the black-and-white film of Eudora Welty
in the visitor center and they love on
their vowels the same way.
Light voices feather stories the same,
Miz Eudora and Miz Louise become one.

Later when I read *Losing Battles*, I've
already met these kin, Louise's relatives,
in northwest Tennessee towns:
my ears smile
with sustained recognition.

Inside the Tudor Revival facade, the guide,
a retired high school English teacher,
slides through Welty's career
and stacks of books teeter on couches
and chairs, and I'm ready for bourbon
then the crab casserole Welty cooks,

no one else in the kitchen according to the guide
who directs us to Lavinia Books, Jackson's
best, where my mother-in-law sips sweet tea
and others lunch. I bob back and forth
between table and store,
helpless in two rooms then Rare Books
under $100.

Miss Eudora's voice
guides my fingers to the Library of America's
Welty: Complete Novels and I'll hear it

on every page, but just now
it rides home in the back seat
and my ears glow in the warm bath.

ON GIVING AWAY MOST OF MY LIBRARY

Spines shine over the years on the full
custom-built 9-foot white bookshelves lining
my outer office, presided over by the framed
print of Munch's *Madonna*, mostly naked,
in post-coital bliss. And that's only A – Ma;
Mc – Z rests on shelves in our old home's
three floors. Well over 2,000 titles,
your basic English professor's library.
Bookworm since ten, I fondle and stack
paper- and hardbacks for decades,
periodic culling not disguising steady
weight gain and in recent years, more first
editions and friends' inscribed books pinch
the shelves such that row ends are shoved
in horizontally, no words in sight.

Strict about my trim shape marking
my aging, imminent retirement forces me
to drastically cut book weight, return
from morbid print obesity as I gift
most of these rows to the local public
library, reserve only what I can't yet disown.
I finger volumes of Conrad and Dickens,
Cooper and Hawthorne and Fitzgerald,
eyes scan my printed surname, acquisition
date, penciled jottings and marginalia
and the sun appears as I remember
the first reading or teaching. I don't erase
but pile and box, freight on a colleague's
heavy hand dolly.

My hands clutch myriad leaves of a half
century, titles from undergrad years
or earlier or from a few years ago
or in between, and I give up pounds
and pounds of flesh, these motley pieces
of my past, a long span of fond journeys.
Will I survive the separation as I trundle
boxes away? Where am I without
their heft, their history? I shrug, eyes
slide off empty office rows, my new core
library re-shelved at home. I step
lightly at the thought of books back
in circulation, free, surviving my body:
my last class.

FINAL DAYS

I upload a last audio
read the final papers
file grades all online

I've stolen into the office
weekends carted dozens
of boxes tossed files

a remote ghost already
though I blink
and the first days

in Montana dance
and before those
a decade in Virginia

when I learned
to teach eventually write
and confidence blossomed.

I relinquish
my role as wannabe
sage, no more captive

audiences, no longer
one who professes,
unsure of what verbs

I will inhabit
in the wide space
before me, my work

voice stilled.

Section IV.

DISTANT GEOGRAPHIES

ON THE ROAD TO HOOPER ISLAND

Days of rain puddle the shoulders
southwest of the refuge. Mist
thickens above the tidal swamps. Loblolly
pine stands give way to Fishing Creek,
narrow finger between Chesapeake
Bay and Hongo River, fat estuary.

Water pools in yards. Bay and river lap
the roadbed. Through the gauze
the arch of bridge emerges, bow
strung from water to water. We rise,
cross to Hooper Island, pass a scarce
string of houses, temporary islands

where the road ends. Inches separate
land from sea as in the Everglades
or Amsterdam without dikes.
The sea level rises twice as fast
in the Chesapeake as elsewhere.
The SUV's tires splash through pavement

under water and Hooper Island settles
in mud, an illusion pausing on its way
to Atlantis, its stand of trees,
like the road, a momentary buffer
before the next hurricane adds
to the rising oceans, the slide of subsidence.

I blink and it disappears in the rain.

JUST CHILLIN'

At *Punalu'u*, Black Sand Beach,
honu, Hawai'ian green sea turtles,
bask just above tideline. Signage
and websites say "bask," claim this dark
beach one of the world's few sites

where *honu* hang out after they feed
on *limu*. Biology explains their "thermal
ecology"; a plaque tells the story
of Kauila, "mystical turtle" who shape
shifts, plays with children of the people

of Ka'u, their "guardian." Above the plaque
on a round disc, a naked girl sleeps
on a turtle's curving carapace; arms
and legs securely cling. A few tourists
crowd the edge of a restricted

rectangle of mounded sand where four
turtles take their ease, oblivious to cell
phone cameras and human desire.
On this turtle island, in our final State,
we follow their cue, doze on sand,

chill beneath hot sun. Here, turtles
show the way. Say it slowly: relax.

THE MANTAS AND US

Among twenty visitors on the *Sea Ventures'*
"zodiac" after dusk in Keauhou Bay, we don
masks and snorkels, jump into the warm
chop, loosely grasp the side poles of long skinny

rafts equipped below with blue cone lights
that occasionally turn white. Styrofoam
noodles balance under ankles, float legs:
a Busby Berkeley choreography of stretched

bodies, our limbs occasionally bump
neighbors'. At Kalukalaehe Point, a self-described
Manta Village created from floodlights
from the old Kona Surf Hotel, the light

concentrates plankton and manta rays,
"gentle giants" unlike stinging cousins,
associate light with food, cluster offshore
in shallow depths. Through the mask, I track

thick drifts of suspended plankton while
a couple of fathoms below, solo manta
rays languidly flap then sail up to the blue
lights, arc smoothly backwards right under

the raft, swim before our wide eyes, white
undersides exposed as their round mouths
gape as they sieve food and their wings brush
fingers or forearms. Their backward arc a perfect

curve, *Moderato*. We're told human contact
damages their protective slime coat yet how
do they avoid raft hordes as they bend
to the light? I read that the local population,

like all of them, drastically declines yet who controls
the flow of us come to watch and gasp?
In this uneasy dance, our lights and numbers
lure the big rays whose easy grace mocks ours.

WELCOME TO POLAND, 1989

In the Europejski Hotel
near Warsaw's old town
soon after our arrival
and weeks after Poland
shook off Communism,
the "electreeznoshch" flickers
out as I register in the lobby.
They echo, "It will come back
on in ten minutes."
No porter.
I haul suitcases to our second floor room
in midday gloom.

I learn *prad nagle sie wylaczyl* ["electricity suddenly off"]

When we check out
the *elektrysznosc* stops, kaput.
My wife stands inside one elevator,
our young son just outside
as she pries the doors back.
Wedged in another elevator between floors
with our luggage, a Pole
who speaks no English uses his cigarette lighter
as though it will shed light.
I still hear our son's cries
down the dark shaft:
one persistent note in a father's playbook
in a distant land.

A THOUSAND POINTS OF LIGHT

In a Polish cemetary, All Saints Day,
relatives wash and brush headstones,
replace flowers and momenti mori,
leave broad flat votive candles burning
in shallow basins atop graves.

In Sopot's Cmentarz Katolicki
my son and I wander amidst the slender
tapers and squat flames in late
afternoon darkness:
low-down lit city as the spirits
of the departed protest slow cold night
like our Yule logs
or fires atop long barrows
ages before Christ.

MOVING ANGELS

Dark angels and fat putti and gilt sunbursts
outline ranks of pipes
in Oliwa Cathedral's
rococo organ case, a glowing alcove.
When we sit during
noon recitals, the organist
flips a switch and the cherubs
twitch and the angels blow
gold banner trumpets that tilt
just back
       and
    forth
as though they warm slowly
to life, one small step
towards us.

Our young son stands on the pew,
grips the back and his eyes dilate
like ours and we're all children
when the carved wooden statues
come alive
and Bach rolls over us
and then *Zimbalstern* sunbursts spin
and bells tinkle
and it's all too much.

Our eyes track and damp down doubt
while seraphim and cherubim
fly to Bach's polyphony whose soaring chords
flood feet and ears while we stare,
hypnotized by heavenly promise
until the visitation ceases

and in the final chord's slow fade
we shake our heads,
sorry to return.

EAST GERMAN TWILIGHT

1.

In the winter of 1990
drab olive military convoys
line East German highways
red stars no longer ascendent.
Their destinations transient,
their uniforms and protocols
precisely spaced,
they motor
into history, indifferent
to their extinction.

2.

In the East German twilight zone
our Polski Fiat passes Trabants,
mini-sedans made out of resin plastic
with cotton fibers
and their two-stroke engines
chuff, a toy putt-putt,
and exhaust spurts in monotonous rhythm,
blue cigar bubbles that dissipate
almost as quickly
as Trabant's reputation.

INSIDE THE WOLF

In our first Polish spring
we drive past Mazuria lakes

then Romek directs us into the woods
by Gierloz and we wander

along overgrown paths lining
fat concrete walls, some atilt, where moss crawls

and deciduous trees careen and bud,
green offset to the rubble of *Wilczy Szaniec*

or *Wolfsschanze* or Wolf's Lair, Hitler's
East Prussian hangout where, I read,

he spent over two years of the War.
Here he planned the Soviet invasion

and, six weeks after D-day, plotters planned
his death in a conference room.

He survived, only to kill himself
about nine months later in his final Berlin bunker.

More than one language floats through foliage;
nowadays, 300,000 a year enter his lair.

Neither *Der Fuhrer* nor any of his flunkies
had seen a wolf but the anthropocentric name

enlarged their fond mirror that reflected
the old German worship of the woods.

Maybe they heard von Weber's sinister music
conjuring his Wolf's Glen in Act II of *Der Freischutz*.

Does this forest differ from those girdling
Auschwitz and Birkenau, where I walked months earlier?

I later learn the retreating SS failed
to blow the place up due to the 8-meter walls.

The forest increasingly masks the concrete,
green and gray capturing the Nazi paradox

of nature worship and state-of-the-art
technologies of war and mass death.

I walk the haunt of this devil—
the world's, not von Weber's—not quite

half a century after Adolf last walked here,
knowing the woods, "lovely, dark and deep"

draw me as much as they drew him,
knowing we can't stay away but also

knowing a green peace eventually prevails.
I smell those stubborn ruins, that luxuriant growth

years later at a small parking lot near Berlin's
Brandenburg Gate when the walking guide

tells us Hitler's bunker lies directly below the pavement
and that now men urinate below a nearby tree.

TRESPASS

At the gated entrance to Ancient Sparti,
"Closed Tuesdays" sign in Greek
and English, my Tuesday anger surges
until I spy the low plastic fence, curled
and bent, beyond the entrance station.

I hop, stride ahead, glance about
until fear subsides and I relax
into my private tour along the Akropolis
past classical and early Byzantine
church ruins, stones from a Temple

of Athena. Atop the ancient amphitheater
I spy a young Greek below who's tracked
me and when we meet he says, "I'm from
Thessaloniki, I followed your example."
I smile as we part and I inspect

the skene and drift back amid old
olive trees with writhing trunks.
I shout inside in late afternoon heat,
the whole site quiet as though waiting
for me to wink aloud my daring.

SPARTAN

I walk down a curling concrete
track past piles of trash to the partly
excavated Sanctuary of Arthemia
Ortheian girded by a tall iron fence.

Here Spartan boys after puberty
were hauled and whipped to test
their endurance. Pausanias,
Roman travel writer, records they

often died, that Artemis's altar
must be baptized in their blood
before she's happy. Tough shit, lads.
The Romans kept up tradition.

I walk the perimeter, strain to see
their dripping bodies and hear
their cries on low stone platforms
surrounded now by tall grass and silence.

IN THE *SENTO*

The old attendant smiles briefly as she hands my son and I
towels and accepts our remaining clothes. With borrowed
geta we step into the main room's steam heat, greeted by
the flash of teeth as several men welcome the pair of tall,
pale-skinned *gaijin*. Their wide grins tincture hospitality
with bemusement, particularly as we take position

at the row's end and lower our bare butts onto small
pink stools before low mirrors and lower washstands,
plastic liquid shampoo and soap bottles cupped in their
holders. Our knees brush our cheeks as this American
father and son, clumsily folded, follow *sento* protocol,
lave hair and body, rinse thoroughly before rinsing

stand and stool before we enter any pool. We join locals
in the small square pools, Alec speaks Japanese by way
of introduction, and I try to match their smiles even as,
in one tub, I flinch from the pinpricks that zap my skin.
We're all in this together and I cast off remaining shreds
of modesty or embarrassment as I nod and forgive

the picture of us,
white and hairy and glowing.

FROM BRIDGE TO ANGEL

My wife and I stumble along the main road
that leads away from the east end of south
Mandalay's U Pain bridge, "the world's
longest teak bridge." After a full day in
central Myanmar heat, we tire, search vainly
for our hired driver or a taxi. I later learn
the driver expected us to re-cross those
uneven slats above mostly dry Taung Tha
Man Lake but our feet never counted on
a round trip. We rest in front of a temple
entrance, watch schoolboys chase schoolgirls
with water balloons, catch them and jam
the balloons down their backs.
Afternoon sinks into a humid gray light
and I sink as my wife shuffles towards
exhaustion. The only Westerners in sight,
we speak few Myanmar words. Strangers
in a strange land, desperation rises to my
tongue and arms.

When we stop in front of Yadanabon
University's entrance, its curved brick walls
and avenue reassure me, as American
academic, a flash of something familiar.
I stop a thin man who speaks no English
but recruits a strolling pair of friends
The attractive woman smiles easily in
her green dress and orders us a taxi
on her phone. An international
environmental law student, she has
studied English for three years and I
see one face of contemporary Myanmar

in her carefully applied lipstick and
perfectly shaped smile and face and
body. She and the two men wait with
us as we wait the taxi. The first man
carries two plastic stools from a nearby
vendor for the big visitors and my wife
sits though pride keeps me on my feet.

When the taxi pulls up, relief washes
over us and we say *kyei zu tin be de*
["thank you"] over and over. I lightly
grasp the student's upper arm, sink a moment
into her wide almond eyes, say "You
are very pretty," watch a slight blush
wash over her face, stretch her smile,
as we sink into the taxi's back seat.

SWIMMING WITH SARDINES

Actually, over them.
I always pried back
the tin's lid,
fingered them out
of their oil bed,
popped them in.

But at Panagsama
Beach my son
and I snorkel
out and the reef
drops to fifty
meters and on
the steepening
slope below
we watch
like God tens
of thousands of
sardines, three
to five inches:
endless swarms
pulsing in waving
lines above the
dim green slope
like 3-D topology,
fluid shape-
shifters who some-
times angle enough
that silver scales
flash in shadowy
light.

My son waves
his arms, a conductor
whose orchestra
instantly stretches
left and right,
violins distancing
from celli. Other
orchestras recede,
swirl. Limitless
schools of fluid
fish shimmer
and I lose myself
in the riot
of flicking fins
until another
admirer bumps me.
When I scan
the surface
dozens of masked
swimmers, mostly
Chinese, crowd
closer from their
boats, together
like a packed school,
and I retreat
to shore.

JEEPNEY RIDE

*Jeepney: the most popular means of public
transportation in The Philippines.*

Long and squat, their sides splayed with kitsch
in lurid colors, diesel engines blow blue from big
tailpipes. Ours parked in Bontoc just off the main
road, mid-morning. We wait an hour, rest under
pine tree's shade near the church school gate.

Another hour. In noon heat we climb in, stoop
narrow aisle to front seat wall, swaddle
backpacks between legs. Those small motions
of immanent departure dissipate. Where's
the driver? My skin prickles as the jeepney fills,

over twenty Filipinos and tall white me. Bodies
touch, my shirt and shorts sweat wet, my odor
concentrates like thick fug. Another hour. Old
folks, teenagers, young mothers, kids sit,
composed, a few murmur, just another day.

I spike inside. When the fuck do we leave?
I can't find the right pace, lack the low gears
to match the bus's. I snap at my guide, close
my eyes, pretend I'm already hiking under trees,
not paralyzed by bodies and bags, the exit

a distant rectangle of blind light. Several lash
gear on the roof, the driver packs betel leaves
and rinses with water, fires up; a few cling
on back steps, the exit blocked, and we lurch
ahead only to stop at a petrol station, one

kilometer. We ride one-and-a-half hours to Barlig,
the jeepney roars through tight curves, engine
echoes off rock walls, air moves, I sway
with packed passengers. I ask the local guide,
"Is there no schedule?" He can't answer.

CONFESSIONAL

"I had an abortion five months ago," Maria tells me
in our Filipino tricycle. "My lover is an architect
and I knew he didn't love me enough. I didn't tell
my parents for two weeks after my 30th birthday."

She says "I tire of the clouds and rain in Brussels.
I much prefer Southeast Asia. I had no idea how
bad it would be. I lost weight, fell sick." Maria declares,
"My father loves me but he's impossible. He only hears
his own opinion. I can only stand being in the village
a couple of days. They can't understand why I travel,
why I love reefs."

"What do you want to do?"
She says "I love diving most of all. I have advanced
certification. I just spent two months in Malapascua.
Only the world underwater is perfect and calms me."
She admits, "Soon I must return to Belgium."

"What will you do?" I ask.

Later, packs on, I hug Maria, wish her *bon chance*.

BUTTON EYES

At the tarsier sanctuary on the island of Bohol
visitors follow directions and reduce chatter
to whispers since sound or motion disturbs
the little guys, solitaires who sleep by day
and cling to an inner branch surrounded
by other branches and thick foliage.

Among the world's smallest primates, not
quite monkeys, their long tails grip behind
stick legs. We step softly to the next volunteer
who points inside, recommends camera
angles. With silent clicks we try to zoom
closer particularly when we spot

their small yoda ears and big round eyes,
bulging buttons that shine, force words
like "cute" or "adorable," pull us as though
we could cuddle these live dolls who cuddle
a branch and wait for our departure
and night, and who might survive us.

EXPLOSIONS

Pinatubo, my guide reminds us, erupted
nearly a month in June 1991: the old
century's second biggest blow that
scooped a crater lake not as deep
as Oregon's and spread a baked lahar
plain visitors bounce across in 4x4's.

As our 4x4 winds down the raw dun
canyon from the trailhead, three bombs
shake our ears and we track widening
plumes. A Filipino soldier stops our
progress as smoke dissipates and
dozens of natives, old and young,

from two villages sprint and scatter
in search of hot metal shards. The
army uses the sere plain for munitions
practice and villagers collect and sell
scrap metal in town, gain many pesos
in this wry feedback loop.

Our driver stops, fingers a warm piece
of bomb which we palm. Soldiers group
around camo trucks, search shade.
Natives used to grow rice along the old
river, now harvest a hot crop hard upon
timed explosions, tiny echoes of

Pinatubo. Booms split the air
from the Pacific Ring of Fire
or an archipelago's army.

UNDER THE VOLCANO

We land at Legazpi Airport, southeast Luzon,
and Mt. Mayon's upper triangle shines
above swirling clouds in dawn light.
Over three days and nights, its sightlines
burn my retinas when the clouds pause
and separate from its mass in their westward

journey. According to legend, clouds gather
at the crater when the doomed lovers,
Magayon, beautiful maiden, and Pangaronon
kiss. They're buried where Mayon rose.
Its calm marks their embraces; when it
sputters, about to blow, the jealous suitor,

Pagtuga, is challenging Pangaronon. Love
or male jealousy, oldest trope. The most
symmetric volcano on earth after Japan's
Fuji-san, Mayon tapers over 8,000 feet
above city and province. I study
its eastern profile, cloudless after dawn,

from an island and gasp, trace gullies
and ridges, imagine the climb. Desire
wells but so does lava and steam
which keep climbers at bay the past
few years. Most active volcano, it
often flares and vents, rarely asleep

for long. Under it I quake, breathe
steadily, place steps, follow my guide
up a new track to its hot spout:

my fevered dream and its broad,
triangle mass loom long
after airport departure.

FINISHING DAVID FOSTER WALLACE'S
THE PALE KING IN THE AIRPORT LINE

My first edition hardcover with white dust jacket of David Foster
Wallace's final incomplete novel sits on my shelf for six years
until I carry it in my faded red backpack abroad then plunge
into the arcane world of the IRS, and I live awhile in Peoria's
Regional Examination Center (REC), 1985, trace the lives of
those bureaucrats who confront numbing numbers and forms
beyond my imagining, and I'm seduced by Wallace, understand
anew his towering rep while his torrential paragraphs surge
through me. Then I'm near its end

when we hastily depart Manila and my wife and I stand in the
EVA Airlines queue in Terminal One two hours before desk
12 opens and I read *Pale King's* final thirty pages, and boredom,
Wallace's theme and our threat, washes over me and I resign
myself even after the line begins to move: I mute impatience,
dwell inside that Regional Examination Center, our brave new
world, while we shuffle forward.

THE MORNING OF THE IGUANAS

— for Kevin Weinner

I picture iguanas scurrying over
rocks or through thick understory

but not high in the canopy.
After breakfast along the raised

wood veranda Kevin spots a green
iguana motionless on a ceiba

tree branch, then several more,
brown bumps scattered across

the Mayan tree of life. I shake
my head when they take sharp

shape through the binoculars.
I later read that green iguanas

live on limbs far above ground
when they mature. Their "third"

parietal eye atop their heads
warns against inbound hawks or eagles.

Their comb-like spines resolve
into separate tines against pale blue sky

and I smile, knowing their secure
niche in the *axis mundi* far above us.

STEALTH RAYS IN PLAIN SIGHT

— for Wendy Ridenour

Below the bar-restaurant dock
in the shallow lagoon
broad-flanged southern stingrays
glide, barely move their wingtips.
Suddenly I see a black stealth
bomber just clearing a rock ridge
when I walk above timberline,
no sound cue for seconds, a giant
bat in a straight glide overhead.

Just below surface these fat
discs swim silently on the prowl
for food, then pause, clamp down
along edges when their mouths
underneath open. One afternoon
as a local stands by the dock
and guts a mess of red snapper,
three rays lap his ankles, eager
for handouts, everyone happy.

When I snorkel beyond the lagoon,
I watch two rays who rest on sand
at right angles: one eyelid slides
open then shut, open and shut.
Don't tread here. I dream of that
dark skirt with its hooded eye
that tracks my slow progress
above the reef.

CIRCLE OF LIGHT

The students and I drift
out of our single file
during the night snorkel.

Torches off, we circle up
clasp hands, lean back
and fin kick to stir

fire algae into frothy
bioluminescence. We
hold tight yet strain

apart, apt metaphor
for human ties as I
tilt back for the brighter

light shed by the drenched
night sky's stream
of stars.

Section V.

HOME GROUND

COMING HOME

Atop Ryegrass Summit on a high pressure
day, the top third of Rainier, fat white mass,
looms above the deep green ridgeline,
shocks the visitor but greets the native,
promise of the snowpeaks and wet
slopes beyond them.

In this early morning light well east
of Moses Lake, the bump of its broad
hump catches me, those three summits
and dark rock bands between glaciers
—Marianne Moore's icy octopus—and
it winks and pulls my heart

as it always has. No setting sun's
spilled yolk, it rises wider and closer
than a full moon as we hurtle westward
and up. John Muir's big snow beacon
forever lures us closer yet never close
enough.

HOME GROUND

When I go west I arc home
to my past beyond the basaltic
scablands: that young range
which takes its name from
a long set of rapids sunk
behind Bonneville Dam in
the Columbia Gorge's constricted
throat. These old wave trains,
lifted by metaphor, extend
far north and south from foothills
to serrated peaks to volcanoes
in a stately procession. White
water rises to baptize my first range.

In my emotional geography, as I
approach the Columbia River
canyon, trails and lakes and peaks
open before me and I sweat and
rise again, half a century of boot
tracks, of mosquitoes and mud
and Devil's Club, of vine maple
and mountain hemlock columns
and pink heather, of curling mist
and rain and sun and meadows,
then steep snow and rock. I
hear plunging waters,
catch my breath.

CHOPPER DUSTER

Outside Ellensburg I watch
a helicopter crop-duster
arc and curve, a giant
bird that rises and dips
and spins and arouses my
envy, confined like others
to pavement and fast lanes
forward. It bombs the field
just moments then continues
its low dance up around
and down. My eyes track
then reluctantly return
to the predictable
straight lane, unable to fly.

OVER SNOQUALMIE PASS

For decades a resident of high dry country,
I hurtle northwest on the Interstate beyond
Cle Elum, bend along the endless construction
zone snaking fake Lake Keechelus's shore
spotted with old stumps, then rise along three
ski hills lining Snoqualmie Pass, that low

hairpin Cascades saddle surveyed by George
McClellan years before his Army of the Potomac
exasperated Lincoln. At Ski Acres I search
for a chubby kid with double lace boots on long
wood skis, years of lessons finally reaching some
grace on snow. At the sharp north bend

I boomerang down the newer westbound lanes
contouring the South Fork's far side, drop
into my wet green past as my parents' faces
float before me and images from childhood
and adolescence surge when I sniff the moist
air or step onto trails leading to lakes or peaks

I once knew. I enter my first geography marked
by endless conifer ranks and low stratus cloud
mats and sheets of rain and slick snow, danger
for inexperienced drivers. But when sunshine
spangles the slopes and the sky rings blue, it's
too good to be true, this Puget Sound lowland

now swollen to over 5,000,000. I, with
out-of-state plates, jostle with the car crowds,
stranger yet not, haunting familiar
sight lines, outsider yet native. Never fails,

that low pass unlocks my past, a giant chest
whose contents loom and glitter as my car

and I descend in the thick flow.

"I WATCH OVER YOU"

I sit on our cabin's front porch, morning
or evening, and stare at Mt. Baker, my

summer volcano which draws words
like feminine, chaste, serene in its white

drapery. John Keeble in *Yellowfish* calls
it a "dealbate and hoary white hump"

that throws its long white shadow
from within, "a dark essence inside

the white cast over things. . .a whirlpool
that pulled things inside it." Instead

of a sinister gravitational center, I fancy
it smiles over our bay and lives, guardian

spirit on the skyline. *Koma Kulshan*
or "Steep White Watcher" watches me

all my life, its flat dome and bell curve
interrupted, on its south side, by its

asymmetric crater shoulder and
Sherman Peak's knob. In day's

lengthening light, its folds and dimples
clarify and it looms closer. It glints,

winks, talks softly about my youth
and age, reassures me in its quiet

presence. My eyes retrace our Easton-
Deming climbing route decades ago

when boots and lungs sealed our
pact. I'll stick with its Lummi name,

pretend it remains silent witness
who monitors my steady return,

whitening hair, gathering wrinkles.
I say thank you as alpenglow blushes

its cheeks and it draws back, aloof
in the night sky.

ON THE BEACH

— for Brian

My folks and brothers always strolled,
rarely plopped on towels
to slow broil;
instead we walked north
more than southeast
searching out agates
or cedar planks
or driftwood art,
sedate pace,
eyes scanning the wrack.

Decades later I pace
this shallow sloped beach
my body has known
threescore years and more
and they accompany me
though dead or distant.

My nose lifts to familiar salt scents,
feet trod familiar carpets
of pebbles or packed sand,
eyes track the bay's perimeter
and foothills and mountains
beyond: my oldest mirror map
for when have I not known it?
This beach has owned me
since chubby childhood.

By some miracle, it remains
largely deserted, its length

tracked by bald eagles perched
atop Doug firs and great blue herons
still on the edge of low tide mudflats
until they razor plunge or take flight
just above the glass surface,
their prehensile squawk reverberant.

Now, silver-haired, I step alone
though not
and Dad, grasping a stout stick,
walks by my side as does Mom
who pauses, stooped, and spots
another agate and their soft voices
settle on my shoulders.
My brothers, one of whom hasn't spoken to us in years,
pace nearby
closer than my wife or kids, now grown
and flown to far places.

I'm a tiny figure in the corner
of this Bierstadt canvas featuring
a wide sheet of water.
My path, solitary
and illusory and secure,
stretches ahead
and generations disappear
and everyone ambles near me.
Their voices seep into the silence
punctuated only by the whisper
of wavelets kissing sand.

How have I nearly reached
my Biblical allotment of seventy years?
On this beach I contain multitudes
including shadows of earlier selves

and somehow, in my sauntering,
I thread decades and geographies.
No matter the distant time zones,
I fly home to this backwater bay
where I'm never alone
and fix the compass of this life
on this beach,
endlessly rocking.

UNBUILDING MY FATHER

For decades the A-frame, sleeping cabin
for two, angled sharply past the tall
shrub beyond the cabin's corner, its gable
a long straight line above salal carpet,
far below our big Doug fir and Western
hemlock, the inverted steep V and cedar
boards bleached from a diet of steady
rainseep and marine air. When I
unlocked the door atop three small
steps, its own must swirled in my nostrils
and I knew I stood only here.

Near but separate, a private sanctum
where low voices didn't creep inside
open bedroom windows. Dad designed,
blocked, sawed, nailed frame, threaded
cedar panels bottom up, fitted small
door window, stretched mesh below
apex. We took turns sleeping beneath
diagonal 2" x 4" braces, sniffed the
faint tarpaper, exchanged confidences.
Once a college friend, Marsha White,
slept in the A-frame but I only kissed

her goodnight, too shy for sex. I
walked into my adulthood as did my
brothers and after more summers,
sons or nephews unrolled sleeping
bags, warmed the hut with laughter
but they too departed and the A-frame
stood abandoned, storage shed of forgotten
voices. Moss surged on cedar, dirt

moistened corner posts and plywood
edges. New owner of familiar ground,
I crowbar soft panels, intent on

replicating Dad's weave, board by board.
I dig out corner anchors, hear hammer
or bar sink into pulp, concede the spread
of rot. Instead of makeover, my brother
and I pry the supports, pummel patches
of siding, break the floor, undoing step
by step Dad's measurements and curses
and sweat. Never a builder easy with tools—
a failed inheritance—my hands touch his
half a century later. I throw down the pieces
he crafted into a fairy tale A, its smell lost

in time's thickening soil.

WATER STRIDER

— *for Le Thu Lodge*

Every day on incoming tide
      with little wind,
she rows her small boat
      or paddles her kayak
and I watch through binoculars.

She calls the salt bay a "lake," claims
      rowing is her *zazen*,
must pull across the water's skin
      daily. Sometimes she
pauses, oars extended, and the
      lapping music of hull
cleaving water subsides. I strain
      my ears, almost hear
her sentences if another boat
      draws close.
She says it's her "addiction."
      I tell her
she lives intimately with our portion
      of bay, supple
membrane that carries sound and
      seals, curious
about this human.

Then I join her, paddle her kayak
      as she practices
with her shell named Louie, bought
      from the City of Seattle.
Her compact brown-skinned body
      releases and extends

and like a water strider, she shoots
        across the glass
surface, pauses as the shell
        slows, then
the sliding seat retracts as does
        her body
gathered for the next pulse of
        legs hips
then arms, only slightly bent.
        She and Louie
work together. She arrows over water
        then stops
momentarily, big oarwings poised
        for further flight.
They're a happy marriage, I tell her,
        as together they fly.

BETWEEN SKINS

Most afternoons I step into the incoming tide,
the bay a mirror, and beyond knee deep,
I swan forward, chill frisson, my head passes
seaweed skeins, nose points to Three Fingers

Mountain as I breaststroke, gather the bay
to my chest, extend arms then circle in, easy
conductor's curves. Shore recedes, no one
interrupts my laving and I tread water, study

our bank's flat V, sidestroke, turn on my back
and surrender, limbs extended, a splayed drift
log cushioned by generous saltwater my body
has always known. In old age I return more

to its sun-warmed surface, poised atop this giant
womb, lose my skin in the space between sky
and sea. When I backstroke, I watch my toes
and the peaks draw back beyond them

and water bubbles in the gentle wake.
I reluctantly leave our old wet haunt and under soft
sun my skin pricks and stretches. I glow
in endless embrace in which I disappear.

Each afternoon I return to break the membrane
that instantly re-knits as I skim its surface.
A harbor seal pauses, watches
my slow passage through the looking glass.

MARINE EAR

When the bay glasses, its skin carries sound long
distances so that I eavesdrop unintentionally
from the front porch above the bank.
Communal membrane pulls strangers close
and I catch snatches from crab pot buoys,
from the knifing kayak or broad-flanged rowboat,
oars poised, or between skier and driver as
the motor winds down. Voices skim the surface,
float up to my command seat as I overhear
what I would prefer not to. Do our topside
phrases travel intact as theirs? Are we
connected through this wide flat ear that
resonates like a cathedral's whispering gallery
girdling an inner dome? I prefer the music
before and after the chatter, when evening
hushes and high tide, a sibilant harp,
strikes a series of soft chords that pulse
and lap and wash over me, loud in their quiet.

POURING MOTHER

As my brother speaks, I work the clip
up the heavy plastic bag that contains
gray grit and flecks of bone. I face
the stern of the borrowed boat, next

to my wife, which our younger son rows.
Hands link two boats a gentle drift
offshore, the other holding my brother,
sister-in-law, niece, and cousin who toss

the clipped flowerlets of white and pink mums
and offer story and comment that capture
my mother. My face clenches and eyes pour
behind sunglasses as my finger breaks open

the bag and I pour Lorraine, a steady sifting
stream, into the bay where, seventeen years
and four days later, she finally rejoins Father.
The eulogies of others, some tearful, offset

my sobbing silence. I flash in and out of our
private ceremony, wracked by the gap
between tongue and heart, my reputation
as wordsmith vanished.

In the stretching silence I mutter "Let's go"
and after we beach and tie the boats, I breast
stroke out in the gathering tide and almost
meet the random constellation of mums

that bob gently towards me in my basin
of tears where, as Whitman knew, we rock
endlessly in our beginning and end and
beyond, from salt to salt.

FAST HATCHES

In the cabin's kitchen, early August,
Lynn and Mary Ann wash bowls of blackberries,
cull on cookie sheets as tiny white worms,
fruit fly larvae disturbed inside their sweet
nest, writhe in air, poke and curl before

our startled eyes as they seek change
and we re-set our vision of the annual harvest.
My niece reads online that in the season's
early higher heat fruit flies burrow and lay
legions of eggs which eye and tongue ignore,

but earlier hatches release larvae
in search of wings, and their blind wriggling
paralyzes our vision, kills our mouth's desire
for cobbler. We concede the field, retreat
to late-season raspberries, store bought,

lower sugar content, and I re-adjust my
taste buds, one flavor of high summer gone.

SPLITTING WOOD

I swing the old maul onto the wedge poised
over a round of western hemlock at the head
of the grass driveway and half a century slips
off. My father says "keep a steady pace. Don't
lift the maul too high. Hit square on the wedge.
Use the least effort to open the wood. Follow
any hairline cracks and watch out for knots."
His soft baritone guides my chubby body

as I learn the sharp strike of maul on wedge,
the swing of the double-bitted axe. "Keep
your legs spread. Face the round directly,
and drop the blade where your eye directs."
My older brother and I split and stacked
quarter rounds for the shallow fireplace,
kindling for the old stove. Now, solo, I
alternate two wedges, open the blond hemlock

sections like orange segments. I think of Frost
with his bum ax helve and his "Wood-Pile."
Hemlock scent along with smoky sweet western
red cedar swirls around my nose and my father,
dead twenty years, stands at my side though
I have reached mid-sixties. I haul the new chunks
with the flat-bed wooden wheelbarrow he built
"hell for stout" and build two decks atop leveled

pole runners. As I dovetail the ends, I no longer
know whose hands place the flat halves.

EVENING VISITATION

I step on the front porch
and the California gray whale
blows and a wet sigh
spreads over the bay and low sky.

Mid-evening, steel wool clouds,
the bottoms bright from shore lights
that bead the bay whose glass surface
pulls sound close in the silence.

The whale fins gently, rolls
and bottom feeds, dimly visible,
and its spouting gathers us inside itself,
baptized by its breath.

MATER DOLOROSA

They carried stillborns around on their backs
until they dissolved back into the ocean.
            —*She's Come Undone,* Wally Lamb

Tahlequah's calf, which she birthed
weeks ago, lived half an hour but
she won't accept death, instead
she carries the stillborn behind one
fin or pushes it with her head, poised
on her rostrum, a thousand miles.

The calf wastes away slowly, still-life
parody driving Tahlequah's fierce
maternity and when it slips her
grip she takes several breaths
then dives deeply, returning with
her body to the surface, and we

hold our breath with hers. Scientists
track Tahlequah and J pod, her
family clan who slowly starve
and drop due to declining chinook
salmon runs. In Puget Sound
and far beyond we're paralyzed

by her grief as she refuses to let go
even as she falls slightly behind
though J pod rallies around,
maybe nudges a chinook towards
her. The research director of Wild
Orca says, "She is stuck in a loop,

we are stuck in doing the same thing,
expecting to get better results."
Tahlequah, Mater Dolorosa, can't avoid
symbol and elegy, poster mother
of decline and fall in the Northwest's
Salish Sea. The scientist says,

"What is beyond grief? I don't even
know what the word for that is, but
that is where she is." When whales
breach and blow, we hover nearby
our sister mammals, so Tahlequah
scratches our hearts through her

obduracy until we bleed as she
carries us all to "where she is,"
where she holds fast against
death and we hold her image,
stuck, as we decide "what to make
of a diminished thing."

ISLAND TIME

Within our wooded retreat above the private beach
we fall into an easy rhythm of bright morning,
warm noon, cooler evening. I cradle the current
book for hours, sweat through a few chores, walk
the beach afternoons, maybe swim in the incoming
tide, sit in Dad's wide-bottomed tall-backed rocker
as the sun declines and lights Cascades snow in detail.
I strain to hear his voice gone twenty years now
and taste the quiet, which he cherished, on my
tongue. Kids' shouts or their parents' voices break
in occasionally, remind me of the general hush
that in my aging resonates ever louder across
the cabin. On the front porch I survey bay,
mainland, foothills and beyond, my life's oldest
panorama, as the sibilance of slight waves
and bald eagles' fluting calls, a descending bead,
wash over me—the sounds of near-silence
in this saltwater place that sink inside and my body
vibrates, an Aeolian harp. Long ago Thoreau
preached "simplify, simplify." Here our days dress
informally, and when our three-seasons life calls us
homeward, I drive off island slowly, eyes wet,
pulled back, reluctant to shed old shorts, quit
the quiet that lifts hearts. Island time, summer's
steady *piano*, lures, an ancient Siren song that
promises peace, not danger. I'm hundreds of
mainland miles away and our leafy hermitage,
tacit and empty, calls from a warmer season.

About the Author

O. Alan Weltzien, Professor Emeritus of English at the University of Montana Western, retired in May 2020, closing out forty years of full-time teaching. Weltzien grew up just east of Seattle and returns with his wife, Lynn, every summer to the family cabin on Camano Island, about an hour north of Seattle. He was educated at Whitman College (Walla Walla, WA), where he received his B.A. in English, and at the University of Virginia (Charlottesville, VA), where he received his M.A. and PhD in English.

He taught at Ferrum College (Ferrum, VA), from 1980 to 1991, then moved to Dillon, MT where he taught at the University of Montana Western from 1991 to 2020. Along the way he's received two Fulbright Fellowships (Poland, 1989-90; Bulgaria, 1997-98), and two University of Montana International Teaching Awards: Charles Sturt University, Wagga Wagga, Australia, 2003; and Universite "Le Mirail," Toulouse, France, 2010.

Weltzien has published ten books and four chapbooks. These include studies of writers Rick Bass and John McPhee; *The Norman Maclean Reader* (University of Chicago Press, 2008); and a biography of Montana novelist, *Thomas Savage: Savage West: The Life and Fiction of Thomas Savage* (University of Nevada Press). In addition, he's published a memoir, *A Father and an Island* (Lewis-Clark Press, 2008); *Exceptional Mountains: A Cultural History of the Pacific Northwest Volcanoes* (University of Nebraska Press, 2016); and *Thinking Continental: Writing the Planet One Place at a Time* (co-editor, University of Nebraska Press, 2017). In 2022 he is publishing another poetry chapbook, *Through the Basement of Time* (Finishing Line Press), and a book of his travel essays, *Walking Off the Well-Beaten Path*, is in circulation.

Obsessed with mountains all his life (though a mediocre technical climber), he still skis in winter and scrambles peaks and backpacks in summer. Weltzien and his wife travel whenever possible. They have three children, two of whom live outside the U.S.

☯

About Cirque Press

Cirque Press grew out of *Cirque*, a literary journal that publishes the works of writers and artists from the North Pacific Rim, a region that reaches north from Oregon to the Yukon Territory, south through Alaska to Hawaii, and west to the Russian Far East.

Cirque Press is a partnership of Sandra Kleven, publisher, and Michael Burwell, editor. Ten years ago, we recognized that works of talented writers in the region were going unpublished, and the Press was launched to bring those works to fruition. We publish fiction, nonfiction, and poetry, and we seek to produce art that provides a deeper understanding about the region and its cultures. The writing of our authors is significant, personal, and strong.

Sandra Kleven – Michael Burwell, publishers and editors
www.cirquejournal.com

Books From Cirque Press

Apportioning the Light by Karen Tschannen (2018)

The Lure of Impermanence by Carey Taylor (2018)

Echolocation by Kristin Berger (2018)

Like Painted Kites & Collected Works by Clifton Bates (2019)

Athabaskan Fractal: Poems of the Far North by Karla Linn Merrifield (2019)

Holy Ghost Town by Tim Sherry (2019)

Drunk on Love: Twelve Stories to Savor Responsibly by Kerry Dean Feldman (2019)

Wide Open Eyes: Surfacing from Vietnam by Paul Kirk Haeder (2020)

Silty Water People by Vivian Faith Prescott (2020)

Life Revised by Leah Stenson (2020)

Oasis Earth: Planet in Peril by Rick Steiner (2020)

The Way to Gaamaak Cove by Doug Pope (2020)

Loggers Don't Make Love by Dave Rowan (2020)

The Dream That Is Childhood by Sandra Wassilie (2020)

Seward Soundboard by Sean Ulman (2020)

The Fox Boy by Gretchen Brinck (2021)

Lily Is Leaving: Poems by Leslie Ann Fried (2021)

One Headlight by Matt Caprioli (2021)

November Reconsidered by Marc Janssen (2021)

Callie Comes of Age by Dale Champlin (2021)

Someday I'll Miss This Place Too by Dan Branch (2021)

Out There In The Out There by Jerry McDonnell (2021)

Fish the Dead Water Hard by Eric Heyne (2021)

Salt & Roses by Buffy McKay (2022)

Growing Older In This Place: A Life in Alaska's Rainforest by Margo Wasserman Waring (2022)

Kettle Dance: A Big Sky Murder by Kerry Dean Feldman (2022)

Nothing Got Broke by Larry F. Slonaker (2022)

On the Beach: Poems 2016-2021 by Alan Weltzien (2022)

Sky Changes on the Kuskokwim by Clifton Bates (2022)

Between Promise and Sadness by Joanne Townsend (2022)

Yosemite Dawning by Shauna Potocky (2022)

Circles
Illustrated books from Cirque Press

Baby Abe: A Lullaby for Lincoln by Ann Chandonnet (2021)

Miss Tami, Is Today Tomorrow? by Tami Phelps (2021)

Miss Bebe Goes to America by Lynda Humphrey (2022)

Made in the USA
Monee, IL
18 February 2023

27424053R00115